Seasoned Romance™

Book One

10 Surprising Interviews with
Age 60-plus Men and Women
Who Reveal Candid,
Often-intimate Details
About Their Secrets
for Loving, Long-term
Relationships

Interviews & Edits by Jeoffrey & Renée Powell

DeLeeuw Research Group

Brussels · Dallas · Seoul

SEASONED ROMANCE
BOOK ONE

ISBN: 145389425X
ISBN-13: 9781453894255
Library of Congress Control Number: 2010915872

For more information, go to
DeLeeuwResearch.com and **FirePointe.com**

Printed in the United States of America

CONTENTS

ACKNOWLEDGEMENTS

EDITOR'S NOTE: We want to thank each of the men and women whose words, experiences and advice are featured in the chapters of *Seasoned Romance*™, *Book One*. Without them, there would be no book, and without their zest for life, there would be even less reason for these pages to be printed.

Permission has been granted by each interviewee for these accounts to be used in this book. Because of the intimate details shared in each chapter, certain details and all names have been altered by mutual consent to maintain interviewee confidentiality. Any similarities to the names, places or experiences of other men and women not interviewed and contracted specifically for this book are coincidental and/or unintentional.

Please note that the resorts and spas mentioned in several chapters are very prestigious and expensive, maintain rigorous application standards, have an extensive waiting list of clients and do little or no commercial advertising; therefore, the resort owners have respectfully requested that we avoid mentioning the name of the resorts for all the obvious reasons. Since a selected number of interviews for the Seasoned Romance™ Book Series have been conducted at these resorts and spas, we have agreed, of course, to honor that request.

There are many deserving colleagues, too voluminous to list, to whom we owe special thanks for advice, transcription work, editing and encouragement. We have thanked you personally and now we do it with heartfelt gratitude in print.

Finally, this book is not the result of a technical, clinical or scientific study, nor is it intended in any way to be a substitute for seeking professional and licensed medical, psychological, nutritional, sexual or behavioral counsel. Instead, this book is simply a natural outgrowth of research in other areas of lifestyle and wellness. It is purely a literary attempt to record the experiences of interviewees for present and future generations, and it is intended solely for the enjoyment, research and inspiration of its readers.

A Note from the Editors of DeLeeuw Research Group

The number of seniors in the United States and throughout the world is increasing rapidly. Back in 1930, less than 6 percent of the U.S. population was over 65 years old. By 1950, the number was 8 percent. By 2011, that number has risen to almost 14 percent. Population experts at the U.S. Bureau of the Census expect the percentage to continue to rise during the next 20 years, reaching 21 percent by 2050. That's more than one in five!

Why?

More to the point, how?

For starters, advances in medical care have enabled people to live longer. Throughout the United States, for example, the average life expectancy in 1900 was 47.3 years. Currently that number is 77.9 years in the U.S. and 67.2 years worldwide. That's an increase of over 30 years expectancy in just over a century!

Also, birthrates in the United States rose dramatically during the 1930s and 1940s. This generation is moving quickly into retirement years, and an even larger number of graying "Baby Boomers" and "Baby Busters/ Gen-Xers" are waiting in the wings. Seniors now outnumber the under-21 generation.

What this means is anyone's guess. For starters, greater numbers of over-60ers seem to be enjoying life more and are adapting healthier lifestyles that often include romance. Those seniors are the focus of this book.

A Surprising Adventure

The Seasoned Romance™ book series, beginning with this first collection of 10 interviews (and more already in process), was birthed from research from other projects for several clients in the wellness and aging industries, the mainstay of DeLeeuw Research Group. In the course of interviewing and sending out questionnaires to seniors about a variety of subjects, one fact continues to resound over and over again—how amazingly young, satisfied, vibrant and even sexy so many silver-, white- and no-haired people there are today.

This is surprising to so many people. Take a look around you. In our popular culture, the so-called elderly are often stereotyped in the most unflattering ways—wrinkled, self-centered, cranky, flatulence-filled, absent-minded, unhealthy and absolutely non-sexual. There are few exceptions.

Yes, there are the occasional newspaper stories or local news features on the 80-year-old marathon runner or the spunky age 65-80 dance troupe. But even then, the references to all the challenges faced by the over-60 age group is given as a background to remind readers or viewers how tough it is to grow older.

And as for portraying aging men and women as romantic in popular culture, you can forget it. For example, other than *Cocoon*, *Steel Magnolias*, *Grumpy Old Men*, *Grumpier Old Men*, *Golden Girls*, *Lonesome Dove*, *Bridges of Madison County*, *The Nanny* and *Blue Bloods*, how many motion pictures and television programs can you remember during the past 50 years featuring seniors who actually enjoyed love and passion in a relatively normal and tasteful manner?

The list, though undoubtedly longer than the few we offered, does not go on and on.

Worse, before the past half-century, heart-felt stories about older lovers were even more nonexistent. Can you imagine a Ma and Pa Kettle flick in a romantic setting? There must have been enough fire in the kettle for them to make 15 children, but there was certainly no more hanky-panky going on between the sheets in any of the hilarious stories in the classic film series.

There have been a few commercials and advertisements in recent years that have been promising. Remember the "He's such a nibbler" commercial featuring a couple, and the man's punch line, "You're next, my dear!" That was kind of sexy, right?

Recent advertisements point to the fact that middle age and older men and women actually do "it," even though apparently "it" somehow involves kitchens that magically turn into steamy wilderness retreats and the actual sex act is carried out in two separate outdoor water-filled bathtubs amidst a foliage-filled park! That has to be both amusing and puzzling to teens and twentysomethings who don't even want to think about the basic premise of erectile dysfunction.

Most of the time through the years, however, most people over 60 who are involved in sex or intimacy on film, TV or print are pointedly portrayed as dirty old "geezers" or lecherous old "cougars."

But in our research, we kept coming across people who were diametrically opposed to the old, time-worn stereotypes. We talked with and read questionnaires from men and women over 60 who were healthier, more involved, happier, more focused and certainly more sexually satisfied in ways that surprised both them and us.

Eventually we decided to explore this "phenomenon" about the intimacy enjoyed by the over-60 crowd and discovered that it wasn't a phenomenon at all. Seniors today, in seemingly greater numbers, are simply deciding that life doesn't stop when you blow out 60 candles, 70, even 80 or more. In many ways, to use a phrase that gets repeated often, "Life is just beginning." You will read about older men and women who can out-dance, out-party, out-work and out-love young people half their age. And the ones who can't out-do often out-enjoy!

The most amazing part is how many seniors have actually become more sexually active than before. Things change. The body shifts. New techniques must be perfected. However, using another oft-repeated phrase, "The most important sexual organ is between your ears, not between your legs." Whether you are over-60 or merely looking ahead and wondering what it will be like, you are in for a surprising adventure as you read the pages.

If you think phrases such as "between your legs" used in the previous paragraph, or even pet names for sexual organs such as "George," "Red Ryder," "her velvet glove," "the rattlesnake" or "the warhead" are a bit racy for grandmas and grandpas (and even great-grandparents), think again. As they opened up to us "outsiders," many for the first time in their lives, some of our interviewees were amazing in their growing willingness to describe what works for them. They often seemed to want to let others know what worked for them and how much they enjoyed being intimate, especially during their golden years.

Naturally, many did not sit down and immediately begin "spilling the beans" about the most intimate details in their lives. Many had to build up a level of trust through several in-depth interviews, and all were guaranteed a high level of confidentiality. After all was said and done, all who have participated in this book seemed to feel very good about helping other seniors understand the importance of living life to the fullest, no matter what a person's age may be.

For all these reasons, we salute these remarkable participants and can't wait for you to get to know them better on the following pages.

Book Basics

Just before you move into the book, let us point out a few guidelines:

- This book is not the result of a technical or scientific study. As mentioned previously, the book was a natural outgrowth of research in other areas of lifestyle and wellness.

- The numbers listed beside each name in the chapter titles represent the age of each person at the time of the interviews. Most of the interviews were conducted within the past 10 years.

- The seniors who participated, for the most part, were healthy, had great attitudes, and seemed very excited about both life and romance. They don't represent "average" in any statistical sense of the word, nor was there an attempt to represent whatever average or typical is. These are truly remarkable men and women, yet they could be your next door neighbors.

- As we were told this paraphrase several times by seniors (with apologies to George Bernard Shaw), "People don't stop having sex because they get old; they get old because they stop having sex." There are obviously many correlations between attitude, wellness and sexual satisfaction, and these characteristics ring loud and clear through each story.

- A majority of the people represented in this book have been married for many years, and some have even celebrated their golden wedding anniversaries. Almost all reported monogamous relationships for most or all of their marriages. A few have gone through several marriages. One person, Franco (Chapter 9), has not yet been married, but is making final plans for a wedding as we go to print. Even though he had never been in a long-term relationship, the details he revealed about sensuality and intimacy for people of all ages, certainly seniors, were so intriguing that we decided to include his story. We hope you agree.

The premise, from beginning to end, has remained very simple: "What can people of all ages, especially seniors, learn from the over-60-age men and women featured in the 10 interviews throughout this *Seasoned Romance*™ book?"

The Seasoned Romance™ Questionnaire®[1]*

In addition to many other wellness areas, we especially focused on these five questions for this book:

(1) What is your age, background and general health?

(2) Is sex still a part of your life, and, if so, how has it (and you) changed over the years?

---

(3)   If you are currently involved in an intimate relationship, how long has it lasted? What has made it last? What have been the best (or worse) parts of the relationship?

(4)   What details about you, your partner and your relationship would surprise people if they knew?

(5)   In your opinion, what is the secret to being a seasoned, sensual senior and what is one story you would like to tell that would help people understand how special intimacy can be to people over 60?

Most interviews were done initially through in-person or print questionnaires, then followed up with in-person interviews. People who participated reflect most geographical areas of the United States, as well as Europe and Asia. This naturally reflects the areas where our earlier research and interview work placed us, but we plan to include a greater diversity of global representation in future Senior Romance™ books.

A Final Word

Because of the intimate details shared in almost every story, certain details and almost all names have been altered to maintain confidentiality. In virtually every interview and questionnaire response, that point was emphasized and assured. Therefore, you are reading the words of people who don't normally talk about the most intimate details of their lives. That fact cannot be stressed enough. Because the words are fresh and candid, the results are often touchingly heartfelt, strikingly poignant and shockingly revealing.

As such, we understand "there is nothing new under the sun" and that many people, oblivious to each other and living in vastly different cultures, can have remarkably comparable experiences. Still, any similarities to other men and women not specifically interviewed for this book are quite unintentional and completely coincidental.

Anonymity has been promised to the participants, so please note that absolutely no letters or emails will be forwarded to any of the interviewees under any circumstances whatsoever.

It is also important to note that the accounts printed in this book, while among the best of all interviews, are representative of many others who may be featured in future volumes if demand is as popular as initial reviews seem to indicate. You may even choose to be a candidate for participation by completing the Seasoned Romance™ Questionnaire® in the back of this book. A selection, permission and additional interview process will take place before inclusion in a future collection.

Let us conclude by emphasizing that this study and the resulting interviews are purely for your enjoyment and enrichment. No medical, marital or psychological advice is implied or encouraged. Never, ever should you consider emulating the health, exercise, dietary, lifestyle and/or sexual discussions in this book without first consulting your medical and/or wellness professional.

Above all else, may you enjoy your best years ever as you become as seasoned and sensual as the remarkable seniors featured on the following pages of *Seasoned Romance*™, *Book One*!

LOREN (68) & SOPHIE (63)
Law & Order

"We've even got friends who rib us at times, implying that we are old fuddy-duddies. We just go along with their jokes and smile. If they only knew!"

—SOPHIE

(1) What is your age, background and general health?

SOPHIE

Loren is 68. I am 63. He has been a lawyer for 44 years and still heads a large practice, though he is starting to turn more things over to the younger partners and has been spending a little less time at the office and in court.

I have never worked outside the home, but have kept really busy with two boys and a girl who are now grown and out on their own. Now I spend a lot of time spoiling grandchildren and great-grandchildren.

We are in very good health. We've always been pretty athletic, even back in school. I was a cheerleader and played basketball. Loren was a basketball player, too, and played on a national championship team his senior year in college. Now he mostly goes golfing to stay healthy. I've always loved him being fit. He's very disciplined about it.

(2) Is sex still a part of your life, and, if so, how has it (and you) changed over the years?

SOPHIE

Five or 10 years ago, I would have never participated in an interview about sex, even though it has always been important to us. I would have been much too embarrassed then to reveal anything about our most intimate secrets, but as I get older, I realize that past generations have done a great disservice by not being more open about what to expect about growing older and ways you can enjoy intimacy no matter what age you are. Both Loren and I are very private people, but we love the idea for your study and hope we can encourage other senior couples to get with it!

Anyway, you asked about sex, and that's what got me talking about why we are so glad to be involved in this study, even though it's pretty unnerving, personally.

Sex, for a long time, was so tied into learning how to be intimate with each other, then having babies and raising a family that we hardly had time to enjoy romance for romance's sake. It's amazing how you start out, thinking that you want to spend all your time with someone, then so many daily pressures overtake you, and you end up just trying to schedule a little time here and there for each other. Plus, as his law practice grew, he had to be so involved with his cases and clients that it took up most of his energy.

We didn't realize at the time—through our thirties, forties and fifties—how little we really focused on each other. We were still very much in love and had lots of good times together, but looking back now, we both agree that it wasn't until the past 10 years or so that we both have purposely started slowing down and smelling the roses, so to speak. Part of the reason is that our children are all out on their own now, and part of the reason is that Loren has been turning more of his practice over to his colleagues.

Specifically, concerning sex, Loren was always quite good in bed—thoughtful and respectful about my feelings, careful about his appearance and grooming and such a wonderful lover—and we both enjoyed having it as often as we could, but it's changed over the years. He's a better lover than ever, but we don't do it as many times as before. I would say that it's better quality now, even without as much quantity. I know I am more in love with that amazing man than ever, and he still flips my switch, as we used to say.

Especially when we were first married, it was usually over pretty quick. That part has gotten so much better as both of us have learned to take our time and enjoy it more.

I know I started to enjoy it so much more once I knew that I wouldn't be getting pregnant anymore. Menopause, for me, was a very good thing. Other than the fact that we have to use a lot more lubricant, since the change in hormones has made me drier, sex is actually better than it's ever been, only different.

To answer your question, I'd say that sex is still very important for us, but like I said, it's quality, not quantity, that counts. And I think we appreciate intimacy and each other so much more now than we did even 10 or 15 years ago.

(3) If you are currently involved in an intimate relationship, how long has it lasted? What has made it last? What have been the best (or worse) parts of the relationship?

LOREN
We met at the university during my third year in law school. She was a sophomore

undergrad who worked several hours a day in the law library. She says she remembers me when I was playing basketball during my own undergraduate years, but we didn't meet in-person until after I was almost finished with school and getting ready for my bar exam.

After I became acquainted with her, we were more like friends than anything—usually talking about basketball and things happening on campus. I was always pretty focused on my studies, and by then I was getting closer to graduating and wanted to make sure I ended up near the top of my class, so I wasn't actively looking for a romantic relationship.

Since she was pretty and perky, and since she came in contact with most of the law students every day, almost all the guys tried to flirt with her and get her to date them. She was wise to the ways of all those eager and amorous young law students, so I didn't even try to date her. Mainly I just tried to be pleasant and congenial to her, and I think she sensed this in me. Plus, later I found out that she had liked me since watching me play basketball back in my undergraduate days.

I guess I could have used that to my advantage, once I knew it, but I never was that kind of guy. I was as competitive as anyone, but I never could understand the whole concept of guys trying to score with girls, merely to brag. That sort of thing was certainly true during my basketball days, and it goes on with law students who should know better, just as much as with any other group of guys. Maybe more so.

Frankly, I had more respect for women than that, and when I had sex with a girl, I wanted it to be very special with someone I truly loved. Anyway, that's the way I treated Sophie, and she seemed to enjoy it that I didn't pressure her.

So after talking back and forth and becoming good friends over Cokes and burgers at one of the local restaurants, I asked her to attend a basketball game one weekend. I took a lot of ribbing from the other guys for being the first law student to actually get a date with Sophie, and I finally threatened to punch one guy who implied that I was going out with her just to get her in bed. Nothing could have been farther from the truth, though admittedly, I was increasingly interested in that, too. Still, it wasn't the first thing on the list!

Sophie was smart, interesting and pretty, too. Her southern accent was so cute. I probably fell for her that first date, but I didn't really admit it for a few more weeks. All along, I had imagined falling in love with someone like her, and when it really happened, it took me by surprise. Always before I had been so totally consumed with basketball and then law school, but things started changing when I met her.

With Christmas vacation coming up, I asked her to ride with me to meet my parents on her way home. She got permission from her folks, and we spent a couple of days together at my parents' house before I drove her over to spend the holidays in her own hometown.

Everything went well. She liked my family, and I liked hers a lot. They reminded me a lot of my own family. By the time we got back to campus, we were head over heels in love.

Even my Mother knew that I was a goner. She asked me if I had popped the big question yet. It sort of shocked me, at first, but it also seemed so perfect and natural for me to do so. I didn't actually ask Sophie to marry me until we met back at the campus, but when I did, she accepted on the spot. I'm not sure what surprised my old basketball teammates and law buddies more—the fact that I asked her to marry me, or the fact that she agreed!

The next weekend we went to back to her hometown for a couple of days, and I officially asked her mother and father in person for Sophie's hand in marriage.

SOPHIE

As you have heard, the best part of our relationship is that Loren has always been such a respectful person. I could see that when we talked in the law library. It was the same when we went on our first date. He didn't even kiss me on the mouth, but pecked me on the forehead. I know it sounds funny, and maybe a little corny and old-fashioned, but I got more excited about Loren's kiss on my forehead than all the kisses from every other guy I had dated—all rolled into one. There was something so intoxicating about him to me, and the respect he had for me only added to my growing love for him.

I saw that same respect when I visited his home the first Christmas. My Mama had always told me to watch how a young man treats the women in his family, because that's a good signal how he's going to treat you. Both Loren, his brothers and his father treated his mother and sisters with such consideration. I fell in love with the whole family from the beginning. I loved to see them joking around and enjoying being together. They were all so competitive, so the driveway basketball games and the backyard football games were like all-out wars, but they were also very good natured about everything.

I also liked his family because they were always joking and having a good time together. I was from the same kind of family. I think that our relationship has been good because we've always had a sense of humor about everything. We've always been able to talk through any problems that come up, and that's important, too.

So much of this I have to give credit to both sets of parents. They were such good examples of how couples should treat each other. In so many ways, Loren and I simply followed their example, saw that it worked, and built on that foundation.

I know a lot of our friends didn't have that example, and that always made me even more grateful that we did.

As I said, I think one of the secrets of our happiness is that he has continued to honor me as a person, not just as "the little woman" who stayed at home with the family. He has always asked my opinion about things and valued what I thought. He included me in every part of our finances and plans and career moves.

In many ways, his respect is one of our most important sexual tools, too. With the way he treats me and all, I'd do anything to keep him happy in bed, and he knows it. I love him that much! Best of all, he loves me back.

Frankly, I'm been so much in love with Loren and am so devoted to him, that I even enjoy seeing him sleeping. He almost always goes to sleep before I do. Sometimes I read historical romance novels late at night, which tend to make me amorous-feeling at times. Often I look over at him, sleeping on his side, lying there so peacefully with a tuft of silvery chest hair sticking out the top V of his pajamas. Sometimes I simply can't keep myself from reaching over and lying against him, stroking his backside and legs. I love it when he turns over on his back, and I can touch his face, chest, stomach and legs. I especially like it when he wakes up and wonders why he is so excited.

Usually I don't tell him what I've been doing, but by then I am so ready to have him inside me I can hardly stand it.

But before I keep going around in different directions, let me get back to your question. Here's the thing: sex at our age doesn't have to just be intercourse. It often does not include him actually going inside me. We enjoy so many other things, too. I enjoy just lying next to him, feeling the heat from his body, feeling him move as he breathes deeply. Sometimes

I think if I was more in love with that man my heart would literally burst.

(4) What details about you, your partner and your sexual relationship would surprise people if they knew?

LOREN

I think people might be surprised at how good we are in bed. A lot of my colleagues see me only one way in the office or courtrooms. I've been a lawyer for a lot of years. People consider me successful, and one of the reasons is that I don't cut any corners. I'm very demanding of myself, my colleagues and my clerical workers.

When I go into a courtroom, I'm good at what I do and have a very good record of successful litigations, but it's not because I'm a smarter lawyer. I just work harder and have a great focus on what it takes to win.

Heck, there are lots of guys and gals who are better legal experts than I am, just as there were always much better athletes than me that I somehow found a way to beat.

I'm certainly not ashamed to say that I've won a lot in my life because I've simply worked harder and was better prepared than the other guy. I'm as focused at this today as I was during a championship game in high school or college. I'm intense because I don't want to lose. I may not always be the best or the smartest, but the other lawyer will never outwork me. I tend to look low-key and unruffled, to the point that my opponents mistakenly think that I'm not interested or involved. Underneath, I'm very, very passionate about what I do and very, very competitive about winning, even though I don't take on near the case load as I did years ago.

It's a little different on the golf course, and I joke around some when I'm out with buddies on the links, but I'm still pretty forceful and competitive. I hate muffing shots, and I hate losing even more—which probably dates back to my basketball days.

I was that way back to the time I was a kid. I looked up to my older brothers and loved being around them, but they were absolutely merciless when we played basketball, football, card games or even tiddlywinks. They never cut me any slack, no matter what we were playing. That forced me to get better or get beat. They were also very good athletes, so by the time I got to junior high and high school, there was a lot expected of me. Mostly I was the one with high expectations. I was bound and determined to do better than they had done. It worked pretty well. I made All-State in basketball my senior year, the same year we won the state championship trophy.

That opened the door for me to be recruited, even by some of the top universities. When I hit the court my freshman year, though, I knew I was in tall cotton. Everybody there had been a high school star. It took everything inside me to keep from quitting, because the other guys were amazing. Thankfully, because of the way I was brought up, I knuckled down more than ever and hung in there. I rode the bench a lot until I was a junior, then eventually was a starter.

As I said, I was never the best player on the court, but I strived to be the best I could be. I had at least one teammate make All-American every year I played in college, and I played against a lot of All-Americans, too. They were all more talented than me, hands down, but I can guarantee you that nobody worked harder in practice or games than I did.

When we lost, I was devastated, and when we won, even though there were several times when I hit the final shot to win, I didn't rejoice too much because I was already thinking about what I needed to do to get better for the next game. I tried never to let my feelings show, which was probably good training for my career as a lawyer, but I'm sure "the thrill of victory... and the agony of defeat," as they used to say on ABC's *Wide World of Sports*, somehow spilled out in my emotions at times anyway.

What I'm saying is that I've always been seen by others, I believe, as extremely focused and maybe even unemotional at times. That's why I'm sure it would surprise most of my colleagues and friends who see me as a no-nonsense lawyer if they knew how good Sophie and I are in bed. I'm still intense and forceful. I want to do my best. I'm competitive. I've gotta win, win, win!

Admittedly, for that reason, sex was more of a performance thing, I suppose, for a lot of years, especially in the beginning. I wanted to be good at technique and making sure that I did things right. I read books on lovemaking. I wanted to make sure that she was satisfied, but I was much more concerned about doing it by the book, so to speak, and covering all the bases...step one, then step two, then step three, then score!

Getting to the final step was like going for the winning basket during the final seconds of a championship game. Nothing or no one was going to stop me. The only thing missing was the cheering of the crowd, but Sophie's excitement and sighs were the greatest applause I'd ever heard.

Maybe it was all part of striving to be the best I could be, which is a good thing, but I had to learn that I wasn't competing with anyone else or even what I thought I should be.

With Sophie's help, I've learned to loosen up a lot and just enjoy the sexual act as part of being together with her, not something that should be scheduled for certain times and graded for performance, if you know what I mean. As we have learned together, it's gotten so much better. I've learned to relax a lot, just have fun and let the good feelings sweep over us, rather than treating it like a race to the finish line.

I give Sophie so much credit for that. And because of her patience and incredible warmth, we've had a great thing going for a lot of years. She thinks I'm wonderful because I've been a good provider and have been able to give her a great lifestyle, but I am the one who owes her more than she could ever imagine. Without her, I would probably be an old, hard-nosed, flinty, Scrooge-type lawyer. Because of her, I'm a husband, father, grandfather and lover, and we have the greatest times, traveling and having fun, but it translates into very good times in bed, whether we are warming up or going for the game-winning shot.

SOPHIE

I agree with Loren that it would surprise people who know us if they really understood what we were like in bed, especially since our children are grown and in their own homes. We often go without clothes around the house, and we sometimes have the loudest sex you can imagine. Yes, this little southern great-grandmother gets out of control sometimes, and it feels good to be that expressive.

And when Loren gets loud, especially when he's revving up for the big moment, oh my goodness, he absolutely blows me away, to use an expression that the kids use today.

Believe it or not, that reserved, buttoned-down, no-nonsense lawyer that everybody thinks they know can turn into a wild animal in bed. I doubt if anyone who knows us would ever imagine in a million years that we are like that. We've even got friends who rib us at times, implying that we are old fuddy-duddies. We just go along with their jokes and smile. If they only knew!

And one of the secrets to our good sex is probably the most surprising of all. I absolutely love his perspiration. I like smelling it. I love tasting it. He doesn't perspire as much now as he used to, but it's still enough to get to me. It's part of him, and since I love him so deeply, it's something that I enjoy very much.

Loren doesn't understand it, and I'm not sure I do, either. Maybe it's because I can have something from him that no one else can have. Maybe it's so sensual to me because it's our own delicious secret, I don't know.

I guess it dates back to when he was playing basketball, since I've never thought much about another man's perspiration—before or since, but I remember watching him playing basketball when I visited the university during my junior year of high school. It was his senior year in college, and it was also the year his team won the national championship, and I was in the field house to see that team play two games during the season.

Both times I saw his team play, for some reason, my eyes were glued to Loren from start to finish. He was tall, obviously athletic, dark-haired and Burt Lancaster-type of handsome, but it wasn't just those things that did it for me. I just purely enjoyed looking at him play basketball. He was always hustling, always moving, so within a few moments after the game started, his jersey and shorts were already soaking with sweat. I don't know why, but Loren's hairy chest and long, beautifully muscled and finely tapered legs, all wet with perspiration, just sent waves of good feelings through me, even though I was 'way up in the nose-bleed section of the field house.

I had never experienced anything like that. During the weeks and months afterward, I often thought about Loren in his basketball uniform when I had sexual thoughts. I could close my eyes and think about his legs, his chest and everything else. Imagining his rippling thigh and calf muscles sent such nice waves of warmth through me.

But I just figured that he was some kind of fantasy. I kept the printed programs from both games that I attended, but my family and friends just thought these were keepsakes from attending the game. They were, but if they would have checked, there was one page that was especially dog-eared as I read about him and wondered if I would ever meet a dreamboat like the guy doing the jump shop in the photo.

I kept those delicious thoughts about Loren locked away in my own little dream world and never told anyone those feelings about him, not even to my best friends. I was actually embarrassed to feel so queasy inside over someone that was obviously a Big Man on Campus and national champion athlete. I figured he had women hanging all over him and would never even give some gawky teenager from a small town a second glance.

As I got busy with my final year of school and my plans for college, I tried to push the thoughts about him out of my mind. I remember going to two more basketball games during on-campus visits, but by that time he had graduated, and the contests weren't the same without him in the line-up.

Then, when I actually met Loren three years later after I went to work in the law library, the sight of him literally took my breath away. I know my face must have reddened when he came up to the desk and asked me about some research materials. It probably sounds like some cheesy romantic novel, but I got weak in the knees and all tingly inside. All I could think about were those games I had seen when he played basketball.

I kept thinking, "It's him! I'm absolutely gonna die!"

I tried my best not to let on how much I was so attracted to him. I was afraid he would be put off if I pushed too hard, so I went the other way, trying my best to just be friendly, but not so interested that he would think I was just another giggly coed trying to snare a soon-to-be-lawyer for a husband.

Inwardly, though, I could barely wait to see him each time, to look into his eyes. I remember the first time his hand touched mine as I gave him books he had reserved, and the electricity and heat I felt during that brief instant were unbelievable to me. The worst thing is that I couldn't tell a soul, certainly not him.

I can remember the exact moment when he asked me to go out for Cokes and burgers at a local hangout near the campus. I thought my heart would jump out of my chest. When our knees touched under the table, I could hardly talk.

Then he asked me to go to a basketball game on campus. It was exciting because our university was the second-rated team in the country, and the number one team in the nation was coming to play us. As if that excitement wasn't enough, to sit beside him and share all that excitement was literally overwhelming.

It was everything I could do to keep my hands off him even on our first few dates. I did everything I could to keep from falling hard, but it was like trying to keep from being swept away like some storybook princess with a real-life prince.

We had sex several times after we got engaged, but it was always in the apartment he shared with another law student, one of those leave-your-towel-on-the-doorknob things, and none of the times lasted long. The best memories started during our honeymoon when we actually had time and space to enjoy ourselves.

We honeymooned at the beach. It was mid-August, so it was hot and the ancient window air conditioners in the motel room could hardly keep up. When we made love, Loren would begin to perspire, and I found that my passion grew just from looking at his shiny skin and touching him as he moved inside me. I remember how out of control I felt as I stroked his hairy chest and tasted his perspiration. I would get all wet sexually when I saw it, and it was almost more than I could stand. He could have done anything to me and I would have gone wild. It was everything I had ever dreamed about and longed for since I was in high school, and so much more!

The only way we did it at first was him on top of me, and I just loved feeling him with my hands as he moved, especially the small of his back and his buttocks as he picked up steam. His perspiration made everything even more erotic as he rubbed against me and I touched him. I could feel the rippling muscles of his legs against my inner thighs, and that added immensely to the overwhelming feelings. So luscious!

He was more than a foot taller than me, so it was hard to kiss while we were making love. I loved nuzzling against his chest hair and touching his nipples with my tongue. I do remember his hot breath coming down on my neck was always such a sultry thing for me, too, especially as he got closer to the big moment and his breaths became more like giant sighs.

I remember the first orgasm I had with him inside me because it was the second time we did it on our honeymoon. Maybe it was because we were both more relaxed after the hustle and bustle of our wedding, or maybe because Loren took longer to touch and kiss and play with me. Whatever brought it on was definitely memorable!

I had read books and heard girl-talk, but he was my first and only lover, so I wasn't totally sure that a woman should feel such a lusty, passionate release. When it started happening, I began breathing such deep breaths and shaking and pushing against him, He must have wondered if I was okay. Believe me, I was okay!

Maybe perspiration, hairy legs rubbing against inner thighs and feeling the small of a man's back don't do as much for some women, but they sure do it for me.

Nothing has changed. If anything, his perspiration and the way he moves and his hot breaths on my neck have become more and more of a scrumptious aphrodisiac as we've gotten older. And I still love touching his back and hips as he moves inside me.

I absolutely love nuzzling my nose and tongue in his sweaty chest hair. My favorite thing to do is when he lies beside me on the bed, face-up, and I touch him all over with my tongue. I especially like to taste his nipples and run my tongue around them, feeling the nipples on one side of my tongue and his chest hair on the other side.

Through the years we've learned what each likes, and one of the things I love to feel is his chest, all wet, rubbing against my neck and breasts and nipples. Again, the perspiration might not do a lot with many women, but it's a personal thing for me. It's simply something that I've always liked about Loren.

Okay, maybe that's not what you thought you'd hear from a 63 year old woman, but it's just the way I am when it comes to this wonderful, incredible sexy man.

(5) In your opinion, what is the secret to being a seasoned, sensual senior, and what is one story you would like to tell that would help people understand how special sex can be to people over 60?

LOREN

Even after hearing Sophie talk about how good it is with us, I'll still be the first to admit that I don't really know the secret to being sexy, much less staying sexy. I'm not sure

I'd ever consider myself sensual, but I'm glad Sophie does.

Personally, I think sex just seems to work best when you let it happen, rather than forcing it to happen or playing some role. Today, if we feel like making love, we make love. If we don't, there's no pressure.

Frankly, there are times—sometimes in the morning when we get up, sometimes during the day, sometimes during the night before falling asleep—where we touch and kiss and suck and lick and nibble for 30 minutes or an hour and never actually have intercourse.

If you would have told me 30 years or so ago that I would say that I enjoyed playing with Sophie for a half-hour or more and sometimes not finishing it off, I would have told you that you were crazy. But it's true. It seems very natural. There's simply no pressure. Sometimes it's more fun to build up to intercourse over a day or two or three.

Another thing we like to do is take showers and baths together. We even remodeled the home we own now so the shower in the master bathroom is extra-sized. We wanted it plenty large for both of us to take showers and baths together when we wanted to. The spa bathtub is the largest I could find. Either way, showering or in the whirlpool, being together is very enjoyable.

It is wonderful to spend a half-hour or so touching, spreading suds all over each other and watching the watery bubbles on Sophie's beautiful body. I love sitting down on the built-in granite seat in the shower, with her still standing up, and pulling her body close to me. With the difference in our height, her nipples are level with my mouth when I'm sitting and she's standing. It's such a great feeling caressing her breasts and at the same time roaming all over her body with my hands.

Doing all this in the shower is an incredibly erotic experience. Plus, as Sophie jokes sometimes, when I get excited in the shower, at least she's got a handy place to hang the washcloth!

And when we are in the whirlpool bathtub together, the sparks sometimes really fly. There is something very good about making love in water, especially as the spa jets shoot water all over you. Rocking away in the water can be dangerous, in terms of making waves and splashing water out sometimes, but it's sure worth any cleanup that we have to do later.

Seriously, if Sophie has taught me anything, it is that sex isn't about just a lot of hard breathing and ejaculations. It's more about learning what your partner likes and then doing everything you can to make her happy. And having fun together!

Sometimes she can get more turned on when I give her a backrub or do the dishes and soap her back in the shower than when I actually pursue sex with her. And I'll never understand the thing she has about the perspiration on my body or clothes, but if it gets her engine running, I'm all for it. Put the pedal to the metal, as hot-rodders used to say back in our teenage years.

SOPHIE

Concerning a story that shows how good sex can be for people our age, that's a hard one, for we have had a lot of good times since we crossed the big six-oh.

One of the best times during the past few years was after my sixtieth birthday party. He invited a lot of our family members in for the weekend, and we had a big reception at our church fellowship hall.

It was a surprise birthday party, but I had found out about it. What I didn't know was what else he had planned. He had a limousine pick us up in front of the church that whisked us off to the airport. We flew up to New York City where he had another limousine waiting to pick us up. We went to a popular Broadway musical that I had been hoping to see, to dinner at a nearby restaurant that has been a favorite for years, then onto a suite at a historic hotel where we have stayed several times in the past. Loren knows how much I love it there.

In the main room of the suite was a fireplace with the fire already crackling. When we got inside, he sat me on the plush couch next to the fire and began undressing me, one piece of clothing at a time. I love it when he takes his time because I can tell that it takes every bit of determination on his part not to start ripping things off and getting on with the show.

On this particular occasion, as he sometimes does, he left my silk stockings on. For some reason he loves the stockings and garter belt better than pantyhose, so I usually wear it that way when I get dressed up, if for no other reason that to know he's thinking about it under whatever dress I'm wearing.

When I was completely nude except for the stockings, he went into one of the closets and pulled out a big garment hanger. He unzipped the cover and pulled out a white, full-length fur coat. He had this all planned ahead of time through one of his college basketball teammates.

Loren turned out the lights so the only illumination in the room was from the fireplace. He walked over beside me, laid the coat out between the couch and the fire, fur-side out, and took me by the hands to lay me down on the fur.

I know it's not politically correct to have fur coats anymore, but I must say that it was absolutely the sexiest feeling you could ever imagine—all that beautiful white fur against my bare bottom, my backside and those silk-stocking legs. I guess the word I'm searching for is exotic. It felt very mysterious and darkly erotic and terribly stimulating to be there on the fur with the fire flickering nearby.

He towered over me, and as the lights from the fireplace cast shadows over him, he proceeded to undress himself, smiling as he did an impromptu strip show for me, tossing his tuxedo toward a nearby couch like a male Gypsy Rose. It was especially entertaining because he is always very careful and orderly in hanging up his clothes and never just slings them across the room.

Eventually, I couldn't stand the wait any longer. I reached up for him and pulled him down on top of me. The love from his eyes made me feel so secure and cherished.

The fire crackling in the fireplace gave the room such warmth, so Loren's skin was already getting moist even before he went inside me. I not only got to taste and smell the perspiration that beaded up all over the white hair on his chest and stomach, but I got to experience the most sensuous feeling on my backside as his rocking movements pressed me harder and harder against that luxurious fur.

Finally, his warm surges started going off deep inside me. All the feelings and furry sensations swept over me and lasted for a long time until we both fell asleep in front of the fire.

I hope there will be lots of other great times like that one, but frankly I doubt most will be as expensive as what my birthday evening cost. Still, that was one of the most special we have ever experienced because he had thought of everything and planned it all out to make my birthday so memorable!

And the best part is that when we woke up the next morning, I looked over at him. The morning light was streaming into our room. We were still lying on the fur's white softness, both completely nude except for my stockings. Sure enough, some time during the night he had gotten up to hang up his tuxedo, then he had pulled the sheets and comforter off the bed and put them over us. By the time I woke up, the embers had gone out in the fireplace, but as I thought about the night before, a warm fire continued glowing inside me.

Now, we hardly ever do it twice in just a few hours anymore, but he was still asleep and so relaxed, and I couldn't stop myself from reaching under the sheets and touching his body all over. He still didn't wake up, so I took drastic action. I nuzzled him down below, smelling and tasting and enjoying myself until he quite literally rose to the occasion. When he woke up, he had that little-boy-on-Christmas-morning look on his face that he gets when he arises from sleep and sees that I want him to make love to me.

I asked him, "Hey, buddy, you got a problem doing it with a 60-year-old lady twice in one night?"

Okay, technically it was morning by then, but he got the joke. He grinned sheepishly, then began touching me. Before long, he was returning the favor with his tongue, then was back on top of me with the white fur underneath and all the wonderful feelings happening again. Before it was over, I had him finish me off with him on the bottom so he could experience how wonderful the fur felt on his backside as he moved inside me.

That afternoon we sat in the airplane seats together as we flew home, holding hands, with my head resting against his shoulder. I didn't take the fur coat off all the way home. I kept touching it and thinking about how good it felt to make love lying on the coat.

I hope this doesn't sound sacrilegious, but part of the time on the way home I spent thanking God for such a wonderful, thoughtful man, and the rest of the time it was all I could do to restrain myself from touching his legs and chest and even his most private places!

I guess all this sounds pretty strange coming from people our age, but I doubt that we are all that unusual. I hope not. To us, getting older has definitely been good. If anything, we think seniors should become better at being love-birds! We've had so much more practice, and we know what the other one likes.

As you get older and realize how quickly life goes by, I think you tend to appreciate everything so much more than when you were younger. We do. And it certainly applies to intimacy and romance.

GLADYS (65)
Huck & Me

"Huck and I have worked out so well because we give each other something we've always wanted deep-down. We understand our differences and our similarities better now than ever. We don't agree on everything, of course, but he makes me

feel safe and secure, and I keep his once-secure life a little crazy by always look-ing for things to surprise and shock him."

—GLADYS

(1) What is your age, background and general health?

I've just turned 65, the wife of a 75 year old investment banker named Huck, which is short for Huckleberry. I guess it's pretty obvi-ous who his father's favorite character was from the Samuel Clemens' books.

Anyway, Huck doesn't feel comfortable talking about such personal things as we are discussing, but he encouraged me to do so if I wanted. I do want to, for I want to let people know that it's never too late to enjoy romance.

Huck and I met later in life, when I was in my fifties and he was in his sixties. He was married once before, but lost his wife in a car wreck.

As for me, when Huck and I met, I figured I was a hopeless old maid or spinster, as we used to call them. It's not that I didn't want to get married, or that I didn't have several suitors through the years, but I was the youngest of three sisters, and when my oldest siblings left to start families, more and more of the family farm and ranch business became my responsibility. Then my father and mother died, and I took over everything and ran it like my parents would have wanted.

I don't mean to imply that farming and ranching was something I was forced to do. I thoroughly enjoyed running the operation. Some people are simply born to live on the land, grow crops and work with livestock. I was one of those people, and I knew it at an early age.

Looking back, I can't think of too much I would change. Maybe I would have taken more time for me, but anyone who has grown up on a farm knows how demanding that life can be. Yet I loved it!

Still, I had already started thinking about making some changes and enjoying myself a little more. In fact, a couple of years before meeting Huck, two of my nephews had started working with me during their high school and college years. Both loved the lifestyle like I did and chose agriculture-related majors. It was working out well for everyone concerned, and we began planning for them to take over more and more with our farm and ranch operations after they both graduated. At that time, though, the bulk of the responsibility was still squarely on my shoulders.

What that means is that I hired and fired and did things myself when I couldn't get someone else to do it. I drove tractors, pulled calves, rode horses, mended fences, loaded irrigation pipe and harvested crops. It was a hard life, and lonely a lot of the time, but I did well and earned the respect of both my neighbors and the people who worked for me.

(2) Is sex still a part of your life, and, if so, how has it (and you) changed over the years?

By the time I was in my forties, I had pretty well given up on having a husband and family. I wanted to be romanced, sure, but there just never seemed time for it. I missed having my own children, I suppose, but I always had lots of nephews, nieces and neighbor kids around who loved the animals and farm life.

Looking back, I probably didn't have a lot of time to think about love and romance and being feminine. It's a hard life running a ranch and farm. My hands were calloused and usually nicked here or there. My skin was always dry and my hair stuffed under a cap. Mostly, I wore chambray shirts, faded blue-jeans and work boots. It's awfully hard to be romantic-feeling when you spend all your time running a farm and you look like one of the guys.

On the other hand, I enjoyed feeling sexual. I always did. I had no problem with touching myself and experiencing wonderful and sensual feelings. No problem at all. Like everything else in my life, I figured if it was to be, it was up to me.

I figured I would spend the rest of my life living that way, and I felt comfortable with it. There are a lot of rewards with farming and ranching. It was hard work, but I felt good about life as it was.

Then Huck came into my life and everything began to change. We had a mutual friend, Clifford, a man who had been close friends with my father, who was interested in setting up some of his kids in the ranch business. He and Huck were both from the Denver area, and he asked Huck to come out with him on a trip to look at some farms and ranches in this area. Clifford called to see if they could drop by my place and say "Hello."

I was hardly the picture of loveliness that day. Earlier I had fired one of my best hired hands for getting drunk and wrecking one of our tractors. It had become a pattern, so I knew I had to get rid of him.

Besides that, the moment Huck and our mutual friend drove into the driveway, I also had a truck and trailer arrive with a stud to service one of my best mares. We hadn't converted yet to artificial insemination, which is more common today.

Here I was, all dirty from getting the banged-up tractor out of the ditch, and barking out orders for several other hired hands to help in getting the mare ready.

By the time I walked over and Clifford introduced me to Huck, everything was prepared and the stud was mounting the mare rather vigorously. I must say, with all the mating noises going on, it was a little disconcerting to be meeting someone for the first time and trying to have a friendly conversation.

Huck seemed unruffled by what was going on, though, and I liked him a lot. He was silvery-haired, already in his sixties, but something about him was very youthful, as well. He wasn't handsome, in the movie star sense, but he carried himself very well and his chin was very rugged and square cut. His eyes were warm and friendly. Those things caught my attention, even as I kept dismissing the feelings I had.

When the commotion died down and the handlers were putting the stud back into the horse trailer, I figured that Huck and my friend Clifford would talk business for a few moments, then be on their way. Instead, Huck took me aside, said that he would be staying at the nearest town, and could I have dinner with him that night?

Well, the last thing I had in mind was dinner. I just wanted to finish the day trying to get things back to normal, to make some calls to see if I could find a new hired hand, then to drop into a bathtub filled with bubble bath and finally fall into the sack. Frankly, I was surprised at my own words agreeing to meet him. I had to look hard and long in my closet to find something to wear for a date with a high-powered investment banker from Denver.

That date was very simple, but it was also dreamlike. He brought me flowers—fragrant yellow roses! I couldn't remember when a man did that—probably not since my senior prom. I put the flowers in a vase, then we left for town. He was such a gentleman, holding my chair and everything. After we finished at the restaurant, we drove to a lakeside park and walked beside the water for awhile, talking about my life and his. I felt very comfortable with him—like an old friend, even though I had just met him.

He held my hand as we walked, then he asked if I wanted to sit on a park bench beside the lake. We lingered under the stars talking for nearly an hour, and part of the time he sat with his arm around me. Then he brought me home, walked me to the door, kissed me tenderly on my cheek and left. His cologne filled my senses. He was so manly, yet he was incredibly sweet. I was smitten, I'll admit. All of a sudden, out of the blue, I felt like a Scarlett who had finally found the right Rhett.

Tired as I was, I didn't sleep much that night. I kept thinking of his long legs under the steering wheel and as he sat beside me on the park bench under the stars. I kept smelling his cologne. He wasn't overly tall—six feet or so—but his legs were very long and muscular. I don't know why that excited me, but it did. I found myself wishing that I could see him in a swimming suit, then I even caught myself wondering what it would be like to see him with no clothes on and feeling his legs next to mine.

I kept pushing those thoughts out of my mind, knowing that I would probably never see him again, but those thoughts kept rushing back, making me feel very warm inside. I even dreamed about him when I finally fell asleep that night.

Still, I woke up telling myself, "The last thing I need to worry about is a man in my life. I've got enough around here to be concerned about."

That morning Huck phoned to say that he was going to have to get back home that day to take care of some business that had come up. Admittedly, my heart fell. I thought he was just giving me the brush-off, and maybe didn't like me after all. But before he said goodbye, he told me that he would really like to see me again, then he asked, "Gladys, when are you coming up to Denver? Anytime soon?"

To this day, I don't know why I said that I planned to fly to Denver within a couple of weeks. It really wasn't a lie. I did need to go to Denver. It's just that I hadn't really set a time to go yet.

Later, I confessed it when we spent time together in Denver. He just smiled, and said, "Gladys, that's the nicest thing anyone's done for me in a long time."

I did fly to Denver two weeks later and stayed at a hotel not too far from his investment business. I spent four days there, and we talked and talked as if we had known each other for decades. He told me about growing up on Long Island, then moving to Denver after serving in the Air Force and about marriage to his late wife. He talked very lovingly about his two grown children and his grandchildren who lived on the West Coast. I told him about my parents and family, as well as the farm and my plans for my two nephews to eventually take over more of the operation.

He brought me flowers each of the four days when he came to pick me up. We took long walks through a park near the hotel where I stayed, and again he held my hand as we walked. We went to a symphony one night. On Sunday morning, we went to the Baptist church where he had been a member for decades. The service was somewhat different than this old Lutheran gal was used to, but it was so beautiful being with him, seeing him enjoy the lively music and sermon. Another evening we went to a country club for his friend's birthday party where he introduced me to some of his dearest friends and danced holding me close.

We didn't do anything sexually, but as the four days went by, every time we sat or stood close together, I felt so passionate toward him—feelings I thought had died long ago. I guess they were just dormant, like the wheat seed resting all winter in the ground, getting ready to sprout and grow as the soil heats up in the springtime. By the end of my stay in Denver, I felt like a giddy schoolgirl, falling headlong in love with a man I had known little more than two weeks.

Before we left for the airport, he did the sweetest thing. He took me by his investment firm and introduced me to his large staff as "my very dear friend Gladys," then he took me by his house, a large ranch-style, in a nice area of Denver. After we went inside the house and he showed me around, he took me into the living room, dropped to one knee, held out a beautiful marquise-cut diamond ring and asked me to marry him.

I thought that he really liked me, and I knew I was falling for him. Still, I was hardly prepared for an actual marriage proposal so quickly. I tried to say "YES!" but the words wouldn't come out very clearly. Actually, the thing I remember most, after I slipped the ring on my finger, was dropping to my knees beside him, hugging him and saying "I love you, Huck!" over and over. For someone who prided myself on not being too emotional, I was a goner.

Then he did something so unexpected and tender. He got big tears in his eyes, tears that brimmed over and spilled down his chiseled face. I started crying. We were a mess by then, holding each other and weeping. What a sight we must have been!

For the first time, I think I really under-stood that he felt as deeply about me as I did for him. I guess we were both so used to keeping people at a distance that when we found each other, it was as if we had found real soul mates. I think that's why we were crying, if I had to put words to it.

It seemed so absurd to be happening that quickly, yet so right. For the first time in my life, someone else wanted to romance and take care of me. Even as a child, I had an incredible amount of responsibilities on the farm. That had grown through the years, especially after I lost my parents, that I had become pretty hardened on the outside. I hardly knew what to expect for someone else to be concerned about me.

I'll admit, through the next few weeks, I kept waiting for the bad news—the raging temper, impending bankruptcy, disgruntled ex-wives, or some other horrible skeleton in the closet. I've probably watched too many mystery- and crime-type programs.

But there was nothing! The more I found out about him, the better it got.

We were married within a month and left immediately for a trip to Cancun, Mexico. I had traveled some—mostly in connection with the ranch—but had never been this far away from the farm my entire life, so it was like a world of make-believe.

And when we made love for the first time, it was all I had ever dreamed of and more. Huck was very gentle with this old farm gal, moving very slowly and deliberately. After we arrived at the resort, we went for a long walk beside the beach, with his arm around the small of my back. He kept stopping, putting his arms around me, and kissing me tenderly, telling me over and over how much he loved me and how he could hardly believe that we were actually married. I could barely wait to get back to our hotel room.

I went in the bathroom and dressed in a special negligee and gown. I wanted our first time to be so wonderful, and I hoped he liked me as a lover. I shouldn't have worried. He knew exactly what to say when I went over to the bed beside him. He took me in his arms, kept saying my name, and told me over and over how beautiful I was. I had seldom been told that I was beautiful, but it's exactly what I dreamed he would tell me on our first night.

When he finally undressed, I looked down at his legs and saw that they were just as beautiful, muscular and exciting as I had imagined. Again, I don't know why I liked looking at his legs and enjoyed rubbing myself against him, but it felt incredible. I liked the sensual feeling.

I noticed that the hair on his head was mostly gray, but the hair on the rest of his body was mostly dark. I don't know why, but that seemed so sexy to me, and I enjoyed touching his warm body all over, especially the dark-haired areas. I was a novice when it came to lovemaking, but it seemed safe to try anything with him. I had no problem doing things that were pleasurable to him. I loved the way his eyes closed when I touched his neck and shoulders and chest and firm belly.

I mostly remember his tenderness. He was so gentle as he touched me, then as he went inside. It so felt good to be loved and wanted and held close. I kept asking him to stay on top of me for a long time, and we lay very still with him inside me. It felt full and wonderful to have his maleness there, and it was a feeling I wanted to remember forever.

We stayed in Cancun for a week, and every day he had more flowers brought into the room. It started looking like a florist shop, and I went from vase to vase smelling and touching each bouquet. We swam together, snorkeled, went on boat rides, walked a lot and made love several more times that week.

For decades, I had given up hope of ever finding a man like Huck, and at times I felt like pinching myself to make sure I wasn't dreaming. Cancun with Huck seemed so far away from my farm and ranch, and to me it seemed like paradise to be with a man who loved me so deeply.

(3) If you are currently involved in an intimate relationship, how long has it lasted? What has made it last? What have been the best (or worse) parts of the relationship?

We have been married now almost 10 years. What started out very nice has gotten even better and much more exciting through the years.

Even during the honeymoon in Cancun, Huck begin drawing things out of me as he romanced me and helped me to learn how to enjoy sex. Again, I was a total novice, but he was the most patient teacher. He knew exactly where to touch me, and we both enjoyed it immensely when his fingers found the right places. I couldn't hold back the sounds that let him know that he was doing it perfectly. He seemed to be so masterful, and I melted in his arms every time we made love. Beyond that, I felt overpowered by his manliness. Even his cologne drove me to the moon. I liked everything about him.

We spent some time apart during the first two years as I began turning more and more of the ranch over to my two nephews. During that time it got to the place that Huck and I could hardly stand to be away from each other more than a few hours, much less a few days or weeks. He liked coming down to the ranch to ride horses and help me with the farm, and it was nice to spend the nights in the farmhouse where I had spent so many lonely years. But he was still tied to his investment business in Denver, so those times at the farm weren't nearly enough.

When we were apart, I would spend time reading marriage and romance-type books, trying to think up ways to satisfy him. I often lay in my bed at night, dreaming of the next time I would be able to feel Huck's long legs moving against me.

Once I gave complete reins of the ranch over to my nephews, I was pretty much free to spend all my time in Denver. And we have made the most of it. He has since sold the investment firm to be with me full-time. We travel a lot, both driving and flying. For a guy who spent most of his life inside boardrooms and offices, he has turned into a real outdoorsman.

We have two registered quarter-horses, but they are boarded at stables a few miles from our home—I told him that I had taken care of horses and livestock much too long, and I wanted someone else to brush and feed them for a change so I can just enjoy riding. Huck had never ridden too much, but he has become a good rider, and we have even found a few places within a few miles from the stables where we can ride, enjoy picnics and each other. And having such a grand view of the Rockies as we ride is almost overpowering.

Huck spent most of his life involved with business, rather than doing a lot of outdoorsy things, but he has grown to love fishing in mountain brooks during the summer, hunting game in Canada during the fall, skiing during the winter and going deep-sea fishing in the Gulf during the spring.

I really never had a lot of time to go hunting, fishing or skiing myself, but I've learned to enjoy all these activities, too. I dearly love to be with him and go wherever he goes. I especially love it because all the outdoorsy things seem to invigorate him sexually more than I can say, and our times in bed at the lodges and resort hotels are often spectacular.

I guess you could say that both of us have spent a lot of the past decade making up for lost time. I guess we've been like sponges since then, trying to please and satisfy each other. It must be working. All it takes to get me started is to watch him fishing or hunting or even working out in the yard or driving our small garden tractor around. He always hired people to do his yard work before, but since he sold his investment firm, he's turned into a gentleman farmer.

There's just something about him driving a tractor around in the yard, especially when he's wearing shorts and I can see his long legs. I don't know if it's because I went so long without a man or what, but I turn into a dirty-minded old gal when I see him like that.

This is how hopelessly in love with him I am: One summer night this past year, when I was sure that it was too dark for any neighbors to see, I went out to the tractor shed as he cleaned up his new pride and joy, a small John Deere tractor. I took him by his hands and led him out into the freshly-plowed garden, put a blanket down where no one could see, and had him make love to me with all the night sounds and smells of dirt around. It was wonderful! He really got into it, too. It felt so good and primitive as we lay out in the yard on the soft soil.

I like it that we are two different personality types. I'm more spontaneous. Maybe it's because I always had to change plans at the drop of a hat during all those years farming and ranching. I'm more comfortable with a lot of change. Huck, after all his years as an investment banker in a three-piece suit, still likes to plan things out a bit more than me. Sometimes I really enjoy surprising him completely, just to see the look on his face.

I guess, in a nutshell, Huck and I have worked out so well because we give each other something we've always wanted, deep-down. We understand our differences and our similarities better now than ever. We don't agree on every little thing in life, of course, but he makes me feel safe and secure, and I keep his once-secure life a little crazy by always looking for things to surprise and shock him.

(4) What details about you, your partner and your relationship would surprise people if they knew?

I don't know about surprising people, but I can think of something that really fires Huck up. And when he gets fired up from this, it makes me crazy, too.

Maybe he associates horses having sex with me, since all that commotion was going on between the stud and my mare when we first met. He says that it was the first time he had ever seen such a thing up-close, and how excited he got as we talked that day with the stud putting the leather to the lathered-up mare.

He talked about this several times, not in a perverted way or anything, but just remarking how interesting it was to him. Finally, one time when we were getting ready to make love, I told him I wanted him to be my stud, that I'd be his mare and that I was all lathered up and ready for him. It was like a game we were playing, and he loved it. I even asked him to mount me from the back, with me lying on the bed with my backside up in the air, and he really got into it. We laughed about it later, but he really, really liked it. So did I. We've played that stud-and-mare game lots of time since then.

Five years or so ago, I was thumbing through a ranch magazine and saw a list of DVDs that included several on horse breeding. I sent for two that looked the best, but one was pretty mechanical and had lots of drawings and statistics, rather than actual horses doing it. The other one, though, was pretty good and showed what happened in graphic detail, including the big moment in slow-motion, no less.

When I put that DVD in the player, Huck's eyes lit up. You wouldn't think that watching horses do it on a video would cause a 70 year old man to get so excited, but within moments he was opening my blouse, sucking at my breasts and feeling me all over with his hands.

He let the DVD keep running while we did it with him mounting me from the back. I must admit that it did something to me, too, to see horses mating. Before long I was begging him to go faster and deeper.

Maybe it's a little strange to hear about something like this, but you have to know the whole story that started back when we first met. Still, I guess it would surprise people if they heard about it. I'm sure of that!

(5) In your opinion, what is the secret to being a seasoned, sensual senior, and what is one story you would like to tell that would help people understand how special sex can be to people over 60?

My answer is to marry a wonderful guy like Huck and buy a horse DVD for both of you to get worked up about!

Seriously, I think the secret of being sexy after 60 is to avoid letting yourself get old and set in your ways. My parents were both like that, even though I loved them both dearly. Huck's first marriage was like that, even though he was obviously devoted to his wife until she passed. And I was headed that way until Huck came into my life. Not being so set in our ways is probably one of the nicest things about our life together.

I think the real secret is to keep trying new things and not getting stuck in a rut. I don't mean just sexually, but that is definitely a part of the whole picture. I read lots of books and historical romance novels to get ideas, and thus far Huck has enjoyed every one. I'm probably more voracious than others, mainly because I knew so little and had no idea of what it took to please a man. Thank goodness for the fact that Huck is a good, patient teacher.

Another thing I recommend—and I would only say this since the reader will never see my reddened face as I talk about such things—is to do whatever it takes to become the very best lover you can. I had a lot of time to make up, so this is probably more important to me than it would be to others. I was voracious in my reading.

Before, you asked for things that might surprise others about Huck and me. And just now you asked for a story to help people understand how special sex can be to people over 60. So I guess I'll give it to you with both barrels, and you can take out anything that's too much over the top.

Since Huck and I have been married, one thing that really helped me to understand and enjoy stimulation both before and during sex came after I saw an advertisement a few years ago for the Eroscillator®. This is probably going to sound like a commercial, but I'll happily tell any gal about this one for free, especially if it will do for others what it's done for me! It's that good. I saw that it was highly recommended by some of the leading sex therapists. It's not just a vibrator, but so much more. The sensations are different from the other vibrating units I had ever used before.

Best of all, it's real simple to use and comes with several attachments for different feelings and uses. I never felt such intense orgasms in my entire life before I got this. That's why I'm so sold on it. Huck has seen it in action lots of times and knows it works wonders on me, so he loves using it to set me off, mainly because he knows I'll be primed and ready when he comes inside. I've even reached down between my legs and used it on my clitoris while he goes inside me doggy-style. All I can tell you is to get ready for making lots of noise and being totally out of control when you do it this way.

(EDITORS' NOTE: We had heard of the Eroscillator® many times before during research and interviews, especially with glowing recommendations from women such as Dr. Ruth Westheimer and Dr. Sue Johanson. Soon after we completed this interview with Gladys, we arranged

to make the Eroscillator® available on our DeLeeuw Research Group's Website, www. FirePointe.com, and we have since received uncountable responses from both women and men, assuring us that we made the right choice in making this available.)

Wow! I can't believe I've gone on and on about things like this, but since you asked about a specific story that would help people understand how special sex can be to people over 60, I might as well tell you one that happened recently that will probably prove to everybody who reads this that the ole gal has gone completely nuts over the sex thing!

A month or so before, I had read about a special club in a romance novel. I did some research online, then I decided to do something so out of character for me. For starters, I chartered an executive jet for an afternoon. It cost a little money, but it was worth it to see Huck's face when all my carefully-laid plans started to unfold. I drove Huck over to the private airport without telling him what we were going to do. Once we were in the air, I closed the partition between us and the pilot, turned on the stereo speakers inside the passenger compartment, and then opened my red jacket to show him that I had nothing on underneath except my red patent cowgirl boots. When I opened my coat, he saw that

I had several sticky pad messages across my breasts with words written in red marker that boldly told him exactly what I wanted him to do, step by step. I will spare you the details, but suffice it to say that the messages included the name Huck and a word that rhymes with it. Then I had drawn an arrow from each note downward.

Later on we laughed about the fact that it was a good thing I hadn't been in an accident or anything on the way to the airport. The whole get-up and messages might have been a little hard to explain to some very shocked EMS worker!

When I opened my coat, Huck was completely floored. Frankly, I was still a bit shocked that I had really gone through with it. All of this is so unlike anything I was when he married me. He was a little uneasy about the pilot, who was less than 10 feet away behind the partition, but I told him that the pilot couldn't hear with the stereo going.

Ignoring my own step-by-step notes, I got on my knees in front of Huck, unbuckled his belt, unzipped his pants and went over him with my mouth. When he got up for the occasion, I wrestled his pants down, lay on one of the larger couch-like seats and pulled him on top of me. Back at our home I had previously lubricated myself pretty well, so he slid in without any problems, and within a few minutes, both of us were gasping for air, totally spent. At 65 and 75 years old, somewhere high over the area between Pikes Peak and the Royal Gorge, according to my calculations, Huck and I had become proud new inductees of the mythic Mile High Club!

It felt incredible, but I'm not sure if it was better because or the high altitude or just because it was so outlandish, exotic, erotic and daring—four words that would have never applied to me before meeting this wonderful man.

The cost of chartering the executive jet was worth every darned cent just seeing the look on Huck's face when I opened my coat and he saw me nude with the notes and arrows stuck in strategic places. It was also worth every penny to see his look of absolute joy and gratitude as we lay together floating high above the snowy Colorado peaks with him still inside me.

I also know that it sure gave new meaning to that song about the "Rocky Mountain High!" that was popular a few years ago. Huck kept saying, "You are one wild woman, Gladys... you are just one hell-of-a wild woman!"

Has this shy farm gal come a long way, or what?

All I know is that as long as Huck enjoys being my stud, I'll definitely be his ready and willing mare, no matter how old we are, and no matter whether we are on a blanket in the dirt or on a plush jet high in the air.

Well, you asked for a story, and you got a dilly, didn't you? Boy, it's a good thing nobody who knows me will put me and this story together—hopefully, at least.

Let me just end this by saying that Huck has changed my life completely, and I'm going to spend the rest of my life trying to keep him surprised and satisfied—whether it's on the ground or a mile high!

GEORGE & MARY (BOTH 66)
ISLAND LOVERS

"Maybe we had to go through all those years of getting by and sacrifices to finally get to the point where we can enjoy our life now. How we live, communicate and make love today is light years from the way we used to do it. And, in so

many areas of life, it's still getting better!"

—MARY

(1) What is your age, background and general health?

GEORGE

I'll go first with the easy one. Both of us are 66 years old. I served in Vietnam as a kid and was later stationed around the world. I was still in the military when I met and married Mary. When I got out, I joined the police force in Mary's hometown. I eventually became a police captain and held that position for 15 years before I retired five years ago.

Mary was an accountant for years, then retired at the same time I left the police. We have six kids, all grown and with kids of their own and even two great-grandkids coming up now. I think we did a pretty good job as parents. We're looking forward to more years together to enjoy our family.

We're in very good health. Both of us swim nearly every day and we take long walks together almost every evening. I lift weights some and both of us do quite a bit of stretching before and after we exercise. We travel a lot together, so we enjoy life.

(2) Is sex still a part of your life, and, if so, how has it (and you) changed over the years?

GEORGE

I was taught in the military to never volunteer for anything, but I also know that the first question or two is probably the easiest, so I'll take this one, too, and save the tough ones for the smarter half of this couple!

Seriously, sex was always pretty good for us. Both of us were from broken marriages and one-parent families, so when we decided to get married, we both vowed before God and each other that we wouldn't put our kids through some of the problems each of us had seen. That was easy— saying the words. The hard part was actually doing it, year after year. But we made that commitment, and we both meant it. We stuck with it, no matter what happened.

Sex was that way, too, for a long time in our marriage. It was something that was part of our commitment, but it wasn't incredible. I viewed it as more of a performance thing, that I had to deliver the goods and be great in bed or I was a failure as a man. Maybe White guys and men from all nationalities go through that, too, but I think it is especially true for African-Americans.

There is this sexual stereotype of a Black man that is good on the one hand, for it inspires you to want to be great in bed, but it is also bad on the other hand, because it doesn't exactly help you to view your partner as someone with real feelings and real needs. When we got in bed, Mary was more of a sex object than a loving partner, if you know what I mean. I loved her, and she knew that, but I just had this ideal in my head of what a man did in the sack.

MARY

George was like that for many years, but I can't put all the blame on him, for I didn't know any different. We both had sex with a couple of other partners before we met, but we were so young then that we both believed the stereotypes. Our sex life was never bad, you understand, but for years it was just sex. That's not a terrible thing, but I think we both eventually wanted more than just sex. We really wanted love and affection from each other, but we really didn't know how to go about getting it or giving it.

We had a pretty good marriage, so neither of us wanted to rock the boat by talking about what we really wanted. It was easier to just pretend that everything was okay and get what enjoyment we could.

If we had been less committed to our marriage, we might have looked elsewhere for whatever was missing. But we were very committed to each other, even if we didn't know how to get to a better place together.

Plus, we really didn't have too much time to dig much deeper. Both of us were so busy—career, family, church and all. In some ways, all the busy-ness was a welcome relief, for it meant that we didn't have to deal with many of the feelings we were both going through.

Again, I don't want to make it sound as if things were bad. It's hard to describe today, but there was just something nagging in the back of my mind that things could be better. Later George told me he was feeling the same way.

The busy schedule was part of the commitment we had made to make things better for our kids than we had it. Both of us had grown up dirt poor, and we definitely didn't want to end up that way, so we worked very hard to make a good life for our kids and ourselves. All of our children graduated from colleges, and are out making good lives for their own families now, so we succeeded on that point.

At the same time, we gave up a lot during all those years of beating out a living. We didn't often take vacations, especially later on when our kids were so involved in sports, cheer-leading, church camps and other activities. Our vacations were mostly centered around something for the children, but I wouldn't take back a moment of those times.

Here's the point: We never went on a vacation where it was just George and me. There never seemed to be the right opportunity or enough money. We mostly scrimped and saved on luxuries and extras to make sure that we could do things later on. I'm glad we sacrificed, for we have a good life now, but we weren't as close as we should have grown. And all of our sacrifices took a toll on us in bed, though I certainly wouldn't have described it that way back then.

I was always working late, finishing up accounting work, usually long after I got the kids in bed. And he worked different shifts and was always on call, so he was usually bone tired. I don't how to describe it other than to say that we sex was great when we could fit it in our schedules, but even when we were intimate, it was over quickly and both of us were ready to go to sleep. As I've read more and listened to other people talk about this, I've realized that is probably very common among couples today.

I guess it doesn't paint a real great picture, but that's the way it was most of the early and middle years of our married life. Sure, we had times that were better than others, but it was never the kind of intimacy that we have since learned to enjoy. Of course, if anyone back then would have asked us the kind of questions you are asking, we would have told them that everything was great, great, great! We believed it, too.

What changed everything for us wasn't just one or two things, but it was a process that happened over a period of four or five years.

GEORGE

During our mid-fifties, we both attended a marriage enrichment-type class at our church. That really got us started thinking about things and talking some. It was more of a course on learning how to communicate as a couple. In other words, it wasn't necessarily a class on sexual technique. We learned

that communication is at the center of everything in a relationship, including intimacy.
We also learned that neither of us was real
good at saying what we really felt or letting
the other one know what we wanted. Again,
maybe it's a Black thing—women seem to
talk more to women, and men talk more to
men—but frankly I think it's something that
is pretty common in most all cultures around
the world.

It wasn't something that we could fix overnight, but at least it made us both realize that
things could be better. More than anything, it
helped us discover that both of us were having similar feelings of wanting more from the
relationship.

From that point, we both started reading
more books about communication and marriage and sex. Both of us learned a lot about
what makes men and women different. We
started talking more about what makes each
of us feel good during sex—something we had
done very little of before.

As we got more comfortable talking, a lot
of the walls went down. I found that I didn't
have to do all the work anymore. I didn't have
to be this big macho man all the time. I realized that we were both very controlling people, and by always controlling our situation,
I was holding Mary back from being more

active in giving me pleasure. Soon it was evident that she was relishing the role of being more assertive, and I must admit that it was mighty good to see her let go more. Her freedom freed me in lots of ways, too.

We both learned to let go more and just let the entire process of lovemaking and romance wash over us like waves, enjoying all of it, not just looking at it as one-two-three-boom, then rolling over and going right to sleep. I realize as I'm saying this that it seems so simple now, but it was a huge breakthrough when we first started understanding what had been missing.

MARY

Not long after we went through a lot of these classes and books, we went to Jamaica on a one-week vacation—just us, no children, no agendas, no work, no responsibility. Our youngest child had just graduated from college. It was the first time George and I went on a vacation alone like this, ever!

We picked Jamaica because my maternal grandmother came from Montego Bay to New York City where she met and married my grandfather. I had always wanted to visit Jamaica, even though we had no close family there anymore. I never really knew my grandmother, since she died when I was a baby, but my mother used to relate the stories Grandmother used to tell of how wonderful the music and the people and the beaches were in Jamaica. It was like a mythological place for me.

Finally, we were able to go. We had saved for the trip for several years. It couldn't have happened at a better time, coming after the courses and books and discussions. For an entire week, we were like teenagers on spring break in the area around Montego Bay. No one knew who we were, so I didn't have to worry about being a manager or mother and George didn't have to be concerned about his reputation as a police captain. We just had a great time laughing and riding around on scooters and dancing and walking on the beach and carrying on.

It was during that week that I had my first really deep orgasm while he was inside me. Before that, I had a lot of great feelings and tingles that I thought were orgasms, especially when he was touching me with his finger or a vibrator, but nothing before was anything like I experienced in Jamaica. It wasn't something that I felt comfortable talking about to anyone before, so I had nothing to compare it to except a man's ejaculation. So when George came off inside me and I felt those flutters usually at the same time, I figured that it was similar to his. I didn't know the difference until the big one happened the first time.

We never drink much, but both of us sampled a couple of the exotic-looking rum drinks there the first night. By the time we got back to the room, I was feeling pretty loose and free.

I had never done this before, but as soon as we got inside the hotel door, I took all my clothes off, danced around the room to the music we could still hear playing out in the street, and then I started stripping George's clothes off. I'm normally pretty shy about things like this, so he was shocked at first. Not that he minded at all, believe me. I could see it in his eyes and big grin. Then he started going with it and laughing and carrying on, bumping and grinding for me. We were a sight to see!

Then I really shocked him. We usually made love before in the dark, but I asked him to leave the lights on so I could see him better. I pushed him onto the bed after I took off all his clothes and started touching him all over. I had done this before, sort of, but never as passionately, and certainly never with all the lights on. By that time I was getting very aroused.

The nights in Jamaica are so humid, so his dark skin was shiny with perspiration from all the dancing we had done before. I love seeing him like that, and I liked it when I was able to make him big and hard. It was exciting and liberating to be turning him on, instead of waiting for him to do most everything.

When I couldn't stand waiting anymore, I put lots of lubrication inside me and on him, then I straddled him, reached down and slid him up inside me. Then I started moving up and down. It was liberating to be so free and seeing the expressions on his face as he laid there enjoying the ride.

Again, especially before the marriage enrichment classes, we had never done it before with me controlling things. Always before, we pretty much stuck to two positions—-missionary and doggie-style—with him doing most of the action.

I quickly found out that with me on top, I could move around more. It was a whole new feeling. His "warhead" (as we sometimes call it—relating back to his army days, I suppose) reached places I had never felt before, especially a sweet spot deep inside. Within a few minutes of moving, I was feeling something coming over me like I had never experienced. It's happened lots of times since then, but that time at the Montego Bay resort was unlike any other. Honestly, I wondered what was going on, but it felt too good to stop.

In addition to feeling so good deep inside, with me on the top and moving around any way I wanted, the top of his shaft was rubbing against my clitoris with each stroke. With all that going on—the sweet spot going crazy and his shaft rubbing up and down against my clitoris—it was all I could do to keep breathing. It was that intense! My breaths got deeper and deeper, to the point that I couldn't control them at all.

Finally, with me moving faster and faster, we both went over the top together. Maybe because everything seemed more sensitive inside with everything going on, the warm shots from his "warhead" felt so much more wonderful than ever before. I eventually fell into his arms and cried. It was that good! I never felt so much like a woman.

GEORGE

I couldn't understand what was happening that first night in Jamaica when she got up on me and got it going. All I knew what that I liked whatever it was. For someone who had always been in control of herself, she was out of her mind bouncing up and down. I could see her breasts bouncing and her nipples jutting out. Her face looked so happy. It was great! It was just so shocking to me when she got that free.

I was kind of uncertain about it all, because she was pretty much taking over. I did feel good being that deep inside her, or at least it felt deeper than before with me usually on top. I was just laying there letting her do most of it. Being on my back let me use my hands to touch her all over, especially fingering her breasts and nipples, which she really seemed to like. Eventually I couldn't hold back and was pushing and pumping against her, arching my back up and down to make it happen faster.

When both of us popped off at the same time, it was the most incredible feeling I'd ever felt. I thought to myself, "Man, if it's this good in my fifties, what's it gonna be like in the next 10 or 20 years?" Here we were, in our mid-fifties and having the best sex we'd ever experienced.

Of course, when she finally put her head on my chest and starting crying, it took me awhile to handle that. I thought I did something wrong or something. Men don't usually have a clue, especially when a woman starts crying. Finally, she got control enough to tell me what she was feeling. The tears were from happiness and all the good feelings she had experienced for the first time.

As we lay there, I just hoped that it wasn't just the rum or Montego Bay. I hoped we had found something that would last. I shouldn't have worried. Sex isn't in the organs; it's in the head and heart.

(3) If you are currently involved in an intimate relationship, how long has it lasted? What has made it last? What have been the best (or worse) parts of the relationship?

MARY

We both had sex a couple of times before marriage. We got married right after that, and we've stayed together for 37 years. We've already talked about what made it last, which was our absolute vow before God and each other that we would stick together, no matter what.

The best part of our relationship is that we have now become very good friends. We had always been good friends, I suppose, but never as deeply as we have become during the past 10 years.

It took all that process of courses and books and that first week in Jamaica to help us really understand that we could not only be good lovers, but we could be good friends. We could really tell each other what made us feel good and what made us hurt. It really helped when we both realized that we could share our deepest desires and feelings without being judged. That was very liberating.

We don't really have any bad parts, other than both wishing we could have learned in the first few years of our marriage what we've discovered during the past decade or so.

Compared to how good sex is now, we look back and realize that we were content for so many years with mechanical sex—a few kisses, not much petting, George going inside, him going off and me feeling lots of flutters, then a few more kisses and touching before going to sleep. I mean, I was too shy and insecure to tell him how I really felt or that I wanted him to touch me more in certain places. He didn't really understand what made me tick. We simply didn't know that it could be so much better, until we got into the courses and books.

Still, maybe we had to go through all those years of getting by and sacrifices to finally get to the point where we can enjoy our life now. The way we live, communicate and make love today is light years from the way we used to do it. And, in so many ways, it's still getting better.

(4) What details about you, your partner and your relationship would surprise people if they knew?

GEORGE

I'll talk about Mary first. It would definitely surprise people who have known her all these years as a straight-laced account-ant and Sunday school teacher and mama and grandma, that she has become such a red hot lover in bed over the past few years.

One of the things I really like about her is that she has learned exactly the places where I like to be touched and kissed. She also bites—not painfully, but in a nipping, good sort of way. She never did that in the early years, but she has become a master at it. When I'm really getting hot, and when she starts nibbling all over my body, it drives me wild.

Yeah, I think that would really surprise people if they knew those things about her.

MARY

I know what I want to say about George, in terms of what would surprise people about our sex life, but I don't know if it will come out the right way. I've never really expressed it in such a concrete way.

For starters, I'd always heard about women who have a "thing" about men in uniform, and I was definitely one of those women when it came to George. The first time I saw him, he was in his army uniform. I met him at a college homecoming dance. He was visiting his brother who was a student at the same college I attended. We danced together several times, and we spent part of the next day together watching the parade and the football game. All the time we were together, I could hardly keep my eyes off this good-looking man in his uniform. He was from a small-town, like me, and so polite. I loved feeling the fabric of his pants legs against my legs when we sat or walked together. I just loved looking at all the braid and ribbons, and he seemed to enjoy explaining what each one represented.

He wore his dress uniform when we got married that summer, and I felt as if I had died and gone to heaven looking at him when we said our vows.

I always had the same feelings about him during all his years on the police force. Maybe a uniform was just something that I associated with my feelings for him, I don't know. But my heart always quickened when I saw him in uniform, especially when he was all dressed up for a social event or community festivities.

You asked for something that might surprise people. After we got more open in our relationship, I even asked George to make love to me in his dress police captain's uniform. I'll admit that you have to be careful about a few of the sharp pins and all, but it was one of the most exciting times we had sex when he was towering over me with all his shiny medals and buttons.

And since he has retired, I've gotten to the point that I like him to make love to me at least once a week or so with a uniform on. He can still get into his army uniform, so sometimes he does it with his military garb on, and sometimes he does it with his police uniform on. It's become a game, sort of.

Sometimes I like him to leave his uniform on while we are having sex, except for unzipping his pants, of course, and sometimes I like to partially undress him—unbuttoning his jacket and shirt, or pulling his pants down to his ankles. Sometimes one of the biggest turn-ons for me is for him to be fully clothed in a uniform, and then I take everything off, even down to his shoes and socks, then finally freeing his "warhead" from his skivvies.

And while I'm on the subject of things that might surprise you, I should tell you about one of the most thrilling parts of being intimate with George. I don't know how else to tell it except to be pretty blunt and just explain how it really is.

What I really find exciting about sex with George is the way his penis head gets so big—almost out of proportion with the rest of his shaft. I mean, he's built well and all, but it's his head that really does it for me. That's one of the reasons we call it the "warhead." It looks so big and explosive.

And the funny thing is that for so many years, the size of his head was sometimes painful and irritating. It hurt when he started going real fast. We tried different things but the lubricants were kind of messy.

It was about the same time as our first trip to Jamaica that we found a couple of new water-based lubrications that were really slick and covered everything well, but weren't a mess to clean up. What a difference! Almost overnight, sex went from sometimes uncomfortable to very, very good.

Again, I can't explain it. He's not circumcised, so when he gets erect, his dark foreskin pulls back and his even darker head stands out all the way around the body of his penis.

What it feels like, when it is really slick, is sort of like the illustrations I've seen of a car's piston going up and down. It pushes real hard against the walls of my vagina when it goes down, then creates a vacuum inside when it comes back up, actually making a sucking sound, which is pretty sexy itself.

Sometimes I actually dream about his "warhead" as it pulls and pushes against my vagina walls, making that sucking sound. The good part is that I can wake up, reach out and touch that beautiful dark-brown head, and know that it's all mine.

(5) In your opinion, what is the secret to being a seasoned, sensual senior, and what is one story you would like to tell that would help people understand how special sex can be to people over 60?

GEORGE

I truly believe that sexiness is all in your head. You'd have never heard me say this a few years ago, but now I know it's true. I always thought that sex had to focus on the sexual organs. But it doesn't matter what shape or size you are, sex is truly in your head.

I do think it's important to keep in good shape and eat healthy. Both Mary and I have always done that. Long before it was popular to go around in all the running suits you see people wearing today, I was running every-day on the police training field in those old gray regulation sweat suits. Mary always stayed very active and walked several blocks from the parking garage to her office when she was working, and since she retired has started jogging with me, too, at a nearby high school track. We enjoy dancing to everything from the old stuff like Count Basie, Nat King Cole and the Motown tunes, even some of the newer hip-hop things. We both enjoy swim-ming. We mainly stay very active and refuse to sit around getting old. Plus, our grandchil-dren keep us very young just staying up with them.

I think that has made a difference over the long haul in our sex life. Sure, we both have gray hair—upstairs and downstairs. Maybe I shouldn't say that since Mary keeps the hair on her head dyed black, but the gray down below is a very sensual to me. I think I can speak for Mary and say without a doubt that we are sexier to each other now than ever before.

MARY

I think the thing that has always made a difference has been the commitment we've felt toward each other. It's that commitment that kept us going even when everything wasn't perfect. Both of us were in high stress jobs. Sometimes we were almost alone as Blacks in a White world. George was the first African-American to be promoted to police captain in the history of our city. For a long time, I was the only female manager in my company—White or Black—and it was always quite a challenge to know that I had to work harder than my colleagues to overcome the barrier of not being "one of the guys." Still, we knew that the outside pressure didn't matter because we always had faith in ourselves, God, our family and each other.

As to the question about how special sex can be after 60, it is hard to draw just one story. One that stands out to me is a recent trip to Jamaica. Yes, we've kept going back. You can't get too much of a good thing, I suppose.

This was our fifth trip there, so we are getting to know our way around a little better. This time we stayed for two weeks. George and I enjoyed good sex a number of times, but the night before we came back was very, very special.

Late in the afternoon, we packed a wicker basket with food and a blanket. Then we started walking on the beach for at least a half-hour. We found a totally deserted area on the white sand, watching the turquoise water lapping against the shore. We sat on the blanket, peeling and eating fruit grown there in the islands. After we ate some of the other foods in the basket, we lay on our backs, holding hands, looking up at the sunset and listening to the surf. As twilight came, the stars appeared. For the longest time, neither of us said anything. Then George leaned over, kissed me deeply, and without talking, he took my clothes off, then shed his shorts and t-shirt.

We lay on the blanket again for a long time, totally naked, touching and stroking each other. You could hardly see his dark skin in the night, but my skin is lighter, so I was a little afraid for awhile that someone would wander past and see us.

Another part of me thought, "Who cares? This isn't so bad. Here are two gray-haired 66-year-olds, so steamed up over each other that we can hardly stand it!"

Thankfully, we were in such a deserted area that no one came around. We could do whatever we wanted there in the dark, and it felt so free, like two randy teenagers romping on a blanket in the sand.

That night was very special, not just because of the sexual fireworks, but because we lay in each other's arms for several hours afterward, thanking God for each other. I don't know exactly what George was thinking about, but I lay there drinking in all the sensual pleasures that were mixed gently with the exotic smells and sounds of the ocean. It felt so good to be against his warm dark body, hearing him breathing and listening to him telling me over and over how much he loves me. I don't know if it gets any better than that!

HAL (69)
THIRD TIME CHARM

"She held me close for a long time, rocking me back and forth, kissing my ears and neck and mouth, and saying how happy she was that she waited for the perfect man. She said it over and over and over."

—HAL

(1) What is your age, background and general health?

I am 69, a retired truck driver, married to Genevieve, who is quite a bit younger than me. She is 51. I was married twice before. Gretchen, my first wife, and I married when we were still teenagers, and she died from a heart attack when we were both 60. Shelley, my second wife, was a lot younger than me. I was 62 and she was only 25. Our marriage only lasted a few months. Thankfully, my marriage to Genevieve has been much better than my second, and we have been together now for three years.

As for health, I do well. I still enjoy smoking a good cigar once in a while and an occasional sip of Kentucky bourbon, but I eat well and go to a gym religiously three times a week. I wasn't always so interested in fitness, especially through my middle years, but my last two wives were real health conscious, and they both have had a good effect on me as far as health is concerned.

(2) Is sex still a part of your life, and, if so, how has it (and you) changed over the years?

Sex is still important to me, but not as important as it was when I was 18 or even 25. Back then, I could get excited at the drop of a hat. I wondered sometimes if I was a pervert or something.

I discovered the joys of getting my rocks off quite by accident, probably like most other young boys. I remember it like it was yesterday. When I was 13, I was climbing a pole to get over a tall fence near a military base that was a quarter-mile or so behind our house, and halfway up the pole, I felt such incredible feelings growing all over my upper legs and my groin area. Wow!

I never did get over the fence that day. I kept sliding down and climbing up the pole a few more times to get the feeling going again, and suddenly my pants were all wet. I wondered if something was wrong—like I had peed myself or something. Yet I knew it was a heck of a lot more fun than peeing. It felt grand. When I got back down to the ground, I touched the wetness on my trousers and felt how sticky it was. Then I realized, more than ever, how my dick was still hard and vibrating. It felt really good. I felt like I had just discovered electricity or something.

I know this probably sounds funny today when kids learn so much at an early age about sex and they see so much on television and movies, but I honestly didn't know if I was the first person that this wonderful experience had ever happened to. That's how innocent and natural it was.

Thankfully, I was all alone and in a deserted area out in the woods. I climbed the pole again and got the same feelings going. The squirting happened again, and it was even more intense than before. I could barely hold onto the pole.

It was a hot day, and I ran over to a nearby creek to wash my pants off. It was one of my favorite places to go swimming by myself, but I hadn't spent much time there that summer, since I had been more involved in the farm work than ever before.

Anyway, I washed all the wet stickiness off my pants, then left my clothes on a rock to dry and swam around for awhile, trying to understand what was happening to me and wondering whether I should tell anyone else how wonderful this thing was that I had discovered.

And while I was thinking about how good it felt to climb the pole, I looked down and saw myself for the first time in a different way.

Maybe it seems so naïve to say this, but I hadn't really looked at myself in the past like I did then. I grew up in a strict Mennonite home where we wore plain clothes and the women even had to wear a head covering, so sex wasn't exactly something you talked about over dinner: "Pass the potatoes, please... and oh, by the way, what can you tell me about erections and ejaculations?"

In fact, as I thought about what my privates had done, I wondered if I had committed some vile sin or something. It felt so good, and I didn't know what to make of it.

I looked at myself and seemed to see everything with new eyes. It was always something down there that I used to urinate, but I never really thought about using it to do anything else. At our one-room schoolhouse, there were a few older guys that had joked around about things, but it was just goofing around. I certainly didn't know anything like kids do today.

In the swimming hole, in light of the intensely good feelings I had just experienced, I guess it all came together, so to speak. It hit that I was definitely bigger down there and starting to grow blonde hair all around it. Somehow all this new information seemed to fit together in a good way.

While I was standing there with the water dripping down over me, wondering whether I should go back to do the pole-thing again and risk possible eternal punishment for having such a great time, I got erect right in front of my eyes. Wow, again!

Intuitively, I touched it and felt all the good feelings. I rubbed it, then put my hand around it and moved up and down. Then I squirted right into the water. The white stuff floated around on the surface. I kept looking at it, touching the ejaculate, trying to figure out what in the world was going on, and pretty damned glad with what was happening to me—even with all the questions.

Mainly, I was relieved to discover that I didn't have to climb a pole to get the feelings going. I simply had to move back and forth with my hand on my maleness. I tried it different ways, with my right hand, with my left, with both. I tried it with my forefinger and thumb squeezing it up and down. Remarkably, everything felt good. This thing I had just invented kept getting better and better.

Best of all, my new invention didn't cost anything or require any special tools or apparatus. Apparently it worked, no matter whether you were climbing a pole or touching it with your fingers. I spent the next hour or so in total abandon, as if I knew it was much too good to be true, and would be over by day's end.

Before I left the swimming hole, I made two major decisions. First, I decided to never tell anyone about this wonderful thing I had discovered, mainly afraid that someone would tell me that it was wrong. Secondly, I decided to enjoy whatever-it-was as long as it lasted. I didn't know if all the pleasurable feelings would keep happening, or if it was a one-afternoon phenomenon that would be gone forever when I woke up the next morning.

Admitting all of this openly makes it seem even more innocent and natural than the way kids grow up today, but I'm not sorry it happened that way. It was very special and unique to me, not tawdry or dirty. Sometimes I think it was better the way I discovered it, rather than having everything thrown at you like these days in movies and songs and even commercials.

Anyway, the very next morning, I woke up and stroked myself a little, relieved to feel everything revving up again. I couldn't wait to get alone once more after I finished my chores. Sure enough, everything worked fine. If anything, it kept getting better as I learned that it wouldn't go away, and as I learned what kind of strokes worked best.

During the rest of the summer, I did it hundreds of times, I suppose. I did it as soon as I could get by myself in the morning just to make sure that I could still do it, and I would do it several more times every day just because it felt so good. Even though I used to dread the late-night trips to the outhouse, I got so I enjoyed them, as well.

Finally, my dad caught me whacking off one time in one of the barns. I was embarrassed as hell, of course, and he took a look at me and walked back out to the field where he was working. I would have sworn, however, that I saw him grin a little as he turned to walk away.

Anyway, he was more understanding than I thought he would be. That day, not long after he caught me playing with myself, we were working together cleaning out barn stalls. When we stopped to take a break, we stepped outside in the breeze and saw a bull putting it to a heifer. I had seen it happen before, lots of times, but never really made the connection to the fact that humans could do it, too, or that it had anything specific to do with what I had invented (and spent lots of time in research and development) over the summer.

I don't know if it was because I was staring more than usual as the bull finished up and moved on to another heifer, but my dad motioned toward the cows and asked me if I knew what was going on.

"Making calves," I replied.

It was the only way I knew to reply. By that time, the bull was humping another willing cow, his balls bouncing up and down from all the effort. Then he slid off and moved away.

"See the bull's red stick?" I nodded. "It's like yours, only shaped different. He shoots juice inside the heifer, and you get a calf next winter. It's the same way with humans. It's the way the Good Lord made it. It's a gift from God. Use it wisely, for it's one of the greatest gifts you will ever get."

That was it, yet it seemed so right for him to say exactly what he did. The example of animals mating on the farm was the sole extent of my sex education to that point. When my Dad said what he did about using this gift wisely, my mind was racing. I wanted to ask him lots of questions, but I was pretty intimidated and just sat there like a lump on a log.

I've thought about it lots of times since then, rolling the moment over and over in my mind, wishing I would have asked him how it all worked, what the juice was for, if I was normal for what I had done or if it was a sin. I guess it was just not meant to be. Maybe it was simply a door I chose not to go through. Or maybe it was a door that he didn't want to open much farther. Actually, looking back, I think he was relieved that I didn't ask any questions. In fact, having had children of my own since then, I'm pretty sure that he was glad the discussion was over. We all try to explain "the birds and the bees," don't we, but I don't think very many adults are good at it or comfortable with talking about it.

Remembering back, I doubt too many kids are cool with talking about it with parents, either.

All I know is that my father didn't judge me. He seemed very wise and grew in stature in my eyes. It was quite a relief to me that he knew all about this phenomenon, and that it I wasn't perverted or sinful.

When the bull got finished and headed for the shade of a nearby tree for a little rest and recuperation, my father and I headed back inside the barn to start working again. I still didn't have all the answers to the universe, I suppose, but at least I knew that everything was all right with the world, and that what was happening to me was somehow part of an over-all plan. I especially liked the part about it being a gift. What a gift, indeed! In his own soft-spoken manner, my Dad let me know that I wasn't some sort of freak of nature—that the feelings I felt and the act itself were all part of some higher plan. For that I will always be grateful.

That night, as I lay in bed touching myself and re-playing what he said, I heard him and my mother in their bedroom, next to mine, making soft sounds and talking intimately. Then I heard the bedsprings begin to move in a rhythmic pattern. It hit me like a ton of bricks that my parents both knew all about this great mystery, had they had obviously done it a number of times in order to have my brothers and sisters and me!

Heck, I realized, they STILL did it. They were doing it at that very moment! That was literally overwhelming to me.

I was hearing noises that I had never noticed as much before. The rhythm got faster and faster, then I heard both of them murmur together. I heard muffled words, then everything got quiet in the next room.

I looked at the ceiling for awhile, wondering if it felt as good to them to be together as it did when I stroked myself. Perhaps it was even better with another person, but that seemed hard to believe. I didn't have anyone to ask about it, and I danged sure wasn't going to ask any more from either of my parents, nor would I ever let them know that I could hear anything coming through the walls.

Regardless, mystery after mystery was being opened to me. And it just kept getting better.

That was definitely a summer to remember!

(3) If you are currently involved in an intimate relationship, how long has it lasted? What has made it last? What have

been the best (or worse) parts of the relationship?

Gretchen, my first wife, and I were married for nearly 40 years. Like me, she was from a very strict religious family. Our sex life was fine and very satisfying, but it was nothing great. Frankly, I was on the road as a trucker, driving all over from the East to the West Coast, so we didn't have sex more than a time or two a week, just because of my schedule.

When we did get together, our sex life consisted mostly of her lying on her back, letting me do whatever I wanted. I use the term "letting" on purpose, since she never wanted to get too involved in anything, other than "doing her duty," as she called it.

I tried everything during our 40 years together. I bought her books and videos. I even tried to get her to talk to our minister, but she was mortified at the thought. I went to a marriage counselor, then asked my wife to join me. Nothing! She said she didn't want to air any of our "dirty linen," as she called it, and she thought that I should spend my time thinking about other things instead of sex.

Don't get me wrong—she was a wonderful woman, a beautiful Christian, a great mother to our three children and she kept our house clean and nice. She was very intelligent and well-read. Gretchen did everything right, and everyone thought that she was a saint, myself included, but she simply didn't want to let herself get too involved or go overboard when it came to sex. To my knowledge, she never had an orgasm, nor would she talk about it when I tried to broach the subject. When it was over, she would lie in my arms for a few minutes, then usually fall asleep quickly, leaving me wondering what in the hell I was doing wrong.

I have never told anyone this, but I cheated on her at times while I was on the road. I'm not proud of it, since I don't believe cheating does anyone any good. I enjoyed the sex part of the affairs, especially when it was with women who were as excited about sex as I was and seemed to like the things I did. The trouble was that I always felt guilty as hell afterward. I was built well from all the years growing up on the farm, and I kept myself trim and in shape, so I found that there are always willing women around the truck stops and even a few who worked in my company's office who enjoyed a romp in the hay with no strings attached.

Eventually, though, I decided to just play with myself whenever I needed a release, rather than being with other women and risking both disease and the disaster of being caught somehow. Doing myself was a lot less complicated, and mainly I didn't feel any guilt when I returned home. I simply hadn't been brought up to jump from sack to sack, and I knew I couldn't live with myself if I kept cheating.

When Gretchen died, I grieved for her, but in time I also had a hope growing inside that I could eventually find someone who could be great in bed, as well as being a good wife in all the other ways.

A year or so after Gretchen passed, I picked Shelley up on a deserted highway out near Albuquerque. She was a college student at the University of New Mexico, and her car broke down on her way home out in the middle of nowhere. Her old car was a goner, and as the wrecker towed it away, she started crying. Instinctively, I hugged her for a few moments, sort of grandfatherly-like, not sure what I should do. Crying women of any age always leave me rather bewildered. I imagine most men feel that way.

Anyway, I volunteered to drop her off at her hometown, even though it was a couple of hours out of my way. She was very young, in her early twenties, but she seemed very sure of herself in so many ways.

We talked through the night and it felt so good being with a woman like her. As I said before, I was trim and had always kept myself up physically, and she seemed surprised that I was 61. She said she was a psychology graduate student and talked about her studies and plans.

We had sex that night. I think she thought it was one way she could express her gratefulness to me. Those were different times. She simply saw a rest stop coming up, asked me to park, crawled back in the sleeper, and took off her jeans and sweater. She had no panties or bra on, so her come-on smile didn't leave too much to the imagination. I guess I looked as shocked as I felt, so she laughed and said, "Come back here, Grandpop, and show me what you've got."

She laughed again and tugged at my arm. I decided, "What the hell!" and went for it. She was so forward with everything, and I was still a wounded puppy inside. The attention felt good. At the time, it just seemed like the thing to do.

Other than doing myself, it had been over three years since I had sex, and seldom in the years before that. Shelley was hot to trot, as the old phrase goes, and so was I. She really got into it, and that set me off even more. She seemed like such an unusual combination of worldly-wise lover and young woman.

I guess it would have been quite a sight if someone could have looked inside the sleeper. Here was a white-haired, 61 year old man still wearing cowboy boots, jeans and under-wear down around my feet, humping a pretty and lithe blonde college student. She was a sight to behold, perfectly built in all the right places, and I felt like a teenager doing it for the first time.

Everything seemed so perfect, and I remember secretly wishing I had a photo of that moment to make sure later that it hadn't been a dream.

Well, as it turned out, it wasn't as much a dream as it became a nightmare. I didn't know that, at first. She was a hot little number, and we did it again the next morning when we woke up. She kept calling me "Grandpop," and kept remarking how she loved the gray and white hair all over my body.

Believe it or not, we got married that next day. In New Mexico, at least back then, you didn't have to be a resident of the state to get a marriage license, nor did you have any kind of waiting period before you could get hitched.

I couldn't believe it myself. I was like a man on fire. She was like a young heifer in heat. I was pulling an empty trailer, so I didn't have to hurry to get home. When we did get back, I called my grown kids. Needless to say, even though they eventually met and liked Shelley, they all thought I was completely out of my mind. In retrospect, they weren't far from the truth.

I was obviously thinking with the organ between my legs instead of the gray matter between my ears. I think Shelley had some kind of a weird thing about gray-hairs going on. Come to find out, she must have liked doing it with anyone my age or older. I never asked her, psychology graduate student and all, about the Freudian side of it, but all I know is that she certainly made my life interesting for awhile. I had more sex during the next few weeks than I ever dreamed possible, but I was also seeing some red flags flapping in the breeze.

She was a world-class shopper. Let me correct that—she was a world-class buyer. I don't think she bothered with the shopping part. I don't know if she had this problem before meeting me, but if not, she was definitely a fast learner. She spent money like it was water. She talked me into buying her a new red convertible. She ran up my charge cards and started other accounts at stores all over the area.

She gave me all I wanted and more when we went out on the open road together, but when she started making excuses for not going on the truck runs, I started getting a little suspicious.

Finally, I asked one of my friends, a private detective, to check her out the next time I left town for a three day run to Virginia.

When I got back and called him, he asked to meet me at a nearby restaurant. We went back to a table with no one around. I was sick when he told me what was going on. She wasn't a prostitute or anything, and she didn't do it with just anybody, but she simply enjoyed making it with gray-hairs—apparently the richer, the better. He filled me in on details about her with a 60 year old professor at a nearby university, then showed me pictures of her giving a blow job to a rich businessman beside his backyard pool. He was 80, at least, and obviously quite taken with what was happening between his legs. The photographs left little doubt that in each instance the men were enjoying themselves immensely and that Shelley was mighty good at reeling them in—hook, line and pecker—just like she had done with me!

I went by my attorney's office, then drove back home and waited for her to get out of the shower. She came out wearing nothing but a towel, saw I was there and dropped her covering, standing nude in the doorway, as beautiful as always. For a moment, I almost decided to postpone what I had planned, at least for a few moments. Thankfully, my brain won out over my rocks, or I might have never got out of that spider's web.

I led her over to the couch and showed her all the details and pictures I had learned from the private detective. I didn't give her a chance to explain, but simply handed her the annulment papers to sign, gave her a thousand bucks and the papers to the convertible in an envelope and in no uncertain terms, told her to get the hell out of my life.

Here's what is really weird: Still gloriously nude, she signed the papers, took the money, stood up, reached over to rub my crotch a couple of times and touched my chest.

"It's your loss, Grandpop! I could make you happy for the rest of your life. The other guys were just for fun, but it's you I really wanted to be with."

Then she pranced out of the room, her tits bouncing in the wind. Within minutes, she packed a couple of suitcases, went out to her car, and drove away.

I wondered if New Mexico knew what was coming, and whether there would be a good supply of rich gray-hairs to keep her happy and supplied with lots of credit cards.

The hell of it all is that she never made it to New Mexico—not by a long-shot, at least for awhile. She left my house, promptly drove over to the 80 year old businessman's place, and took up with him. The neighbors on either side of his big house later told me that they saw them doing it right out in the open beside the pool, both of them acting like teenage fools in heat. I understand that he died with a smile on his face less than six months later and left her an inheritance worth millions. Helluva note! His kids, some of them two and three times her age, were really pissed that she got so much of the estate, but it was tight as a drum legally, and that was that.

Shelley called me a few times after her wealthy hubby passed on and actually had the audacity to ask if I was interested in getting together again, "For old time's sake." She said, "Hal, I feel like I owe you for all you've done for me, plus I really like the way you ring my chimes when we make love!"

Talk about a babe with big brass ones! She even wanted me to help her invest all that money. Strangely enough, I was tempted for a moment to invite her over, make passionate love and then get down to the nitty-gritty of figuring out where she should make all those investments—for a tidy consulting fee, of course!

Thankfully, I didn't.

Not long afterward, Shelley finally moved back to New Mexico. I understand she now owns property all over the place, including several ranches, a ski resort, and even part interest in a Las Vegas resort. Helluva note!

Shelly, wherever you are, you are undoubtedly on lots of men's all-time great screw list, including mine! Unfortunately, most of us, including me, also made your screwed-him-over list.

I guess I've got long-winded here. Enough about Shelley. Let me finish with Genevieve. It's the best part of all.

I married a younger woman again, but not quite so young. Genevieve was in her mid-forties when we met. It wasn't long after I retired from the trucking business, and I decided to take a vacation on one of those Mississippi River paddle-wheel cruises. I used to read about Mark Twain and all, and I had driven trucks over Mississippi River bridges hundreds of times. Every time I drove over the "Big Muddy," especially in Memphis, it just seemed like riding on the river in an old-timey riverboat would be fun to do someday when I had time.

Finally I had time.

It was a week-long cruise down the Mississippi River, and on the very first night I met Genevieve. By that time I was in my mid-sixties, so I had pretty much given up on having a wife again. That was okay by me. I enjoyed my life, my children and grandchildren. I could take care of getting my rocks off anytime I wanted without having to worry about doing it with a woman who enjoyed wearing the plastic off my credit cards. Still, sometimes I wished for someone to share things with.

I noticed Genevieve the very first moment when I walked into the boat's ballroom. Other than the Texas Two-Step, I'm not much for cutting a rug, but that night I asked her to dance, and she accepted. We danced several times that first night, listened to the band playing and talked for hours. I told about Gretchen and Shelley and my family. I couldn't believe how open I felt with her. If she was bored, she never let on; instead, she seemed to like hearing everything about me.

She seemed to feel the same openness with me. She told me that she had never been married, and had spent most of her life as a missionary schoolteacher to a remote area of Alaska. Over the past few years, she had felt that her time there was ending, but she didn't know what she was supposed to do next. Recently, both of her parents had died after lengthy illnesses. She was an only child, so she felt compelled to move back from Alaska to take care of them until their deaths. Her mother had died three months before, and her father had passed away less than a month before we met.

The cruise, she told me, was a present to herself and a way of getting away from the sadness. She wasn't ready for Acapulco or the Caribbean, but she wanted to spend the time out on the river away from everything familiar to her, sorting through her life, trying to figure out what was ahead for her.

By the end of that evening, I knew I had fallen headlong in love with Genevieve. I felt like an 18-year-old all over again. I didn't know if she felt what I did, and I didn't want to push her, so I didn't even kiss her good-night when I walked her back to her room.

The next day I walked around the river-boat, hoping to see her. I almost called her room several times, but I didn't because I was reluctant to intrude or seem too forward. My heart leapt when she finally walked into the stateroom for dinner. Our eyes met, and I knew right then, even before she smiled brightly and started walking toward me, that I was helplessly and hopelessly in love with her. It scared me, for I kept thinking of the huge mistake I had made by being so impulsive with Shelley.

We talked again for hours. That night I kissed her goodnight. Just for a moment. Nothing more. The next day we spent all day together on the decks, watching the gorgeous scenery as it drifted past, talking and laughing.

Again, I was more like a 14 year old boy with fuzzy blonde pubic hair, trying to understand what the hell was happening, rather than a crusty 65 year old white-haired man who should have more sense. So much for control and wisdom!

I guess my main problem, all my life, is that I have been a hopeless romantic. I've always enjoyed reading stories or going to Cary Grant- or Tom Hanks-type movies where the leading man sweeps the woman off her feet and they love each other passionately, happily ever after.

I had never got that before—not from Gretchen and certainly not from Shelley. I had even reached the point where I figured it had to be my fault. Maybe it was meant to be that I would never have all the romance and passion that I wanted. Maybe I wanted too much. Maybe I simply had to be more realistic.

But Genevieve seemed so romantic, too. Even her name sounded like a woman in a romance novel. I loved speaking her name. She seemed to like it when I said it, too.

Finally, on the last night before the cruise ended in New Orleans, I decided I had nothing to lose. Until that time, we mostly danced and walked, hand-in-hand, on the decks, and kissed goodnight at her door.

When it was almost midnight, I decided to tell her how I felt. I told her, bumbling and fumbling all over the place, how deeply I loved her, then I kissed her as passionately as I dared. She returned the kiss, and we held each other for what seemed like an hour. It was really only a few minutes, but I knew right then that I couldn't live without her, even though I knew it was crazy to be falling so hopelessly in love in such a short time. I could only imagine what my kids would say: "Oh, no! Not again, Dad! Does the name Shelley ring any bells?"

Still, deep down, I felt as if meeting Genevieve was part of my destiny—as if all the pieces of life's puzzle were fitting together.

She didn't ask me inside her room, and I was afraid to spoil things by seeking to spend more time with her that night. I kept telling myself that she had spent her life as a missionary schoolteacher and didn't need a lecherous old man trying to get her in bed. She did say that she loved me, too, and she touched my face gently as we kissed several more times. Maybe it was my imagination, but she seemed to press harder against my body each time we kissed. Finally, she said that she looked forward to seeing me the next morning and closed the door gently.

I sat on the deck for hours that night, listening to the big paddlewheel, watching the lights on the riverbank go past, looking up at the stars and wondering if God had finally heard all my prayers and given me someone who could make me as happy as I planned to make her.

We got married two months later, and we have been happier than I ever imagined during the three years since then.

(4) What details about you, your partner and your relationship would surprise people if they knew?

I guess this is a good answer, since it was surprising to me. Even though she was 46 when we got married, Genevieve was still a virgin, and that made our first time even more special and remarkable, since she had waited all her life for the right man. She told me that God had promised her, even as a young teenager, that she would someday be married to a man He had especially prepared for her.

Talk about pressure!

Despite the mistakes I've made in my life, I really did feel as if God prepared me for her, and her for me. I'm no saint, but I really do believe that God directs us when we let Him. Shelley was the perfect example of what happens when I didn't listen very well. Genevieve is the perfect example of what happens when I did.

Anyway, even though she was a 46 year old virgin, or maybe because she was, life with her has been the most exciting adventure. She is exactly the opposite of what Gretchen, which was "allowing" me to do what I want as more of a duty than anything. And I don't even want to bring Shelley into the conversation. Genevieve is in a league by herself, and she's the fastest learner I could ever imagine.

The first night after our marriage, I could hardly wait until we got in the motel room. After we touched and kissed for at least a half-hour, the big moment approached. I put lots of extra lubrication on to keep from hurting her.

I wish I could tell you that my expertise was outstanding and my control was incredibly skilled, but I was so hot by the time I got inside her that I flailed in and out for just a few moments until I went off. Thankfully, she had nothing to compare me to, so she kept telling me how good it felt and how much she loved me.

Again, I felt more like a horny 14-year-old than a guy in my mid-sixties as I kissed her and tried to get my breath. I just hoped that she wasn't disappointed for her first time, since it was so short in duration.

Instead, she held me close for a long time, rocking me back and forth, kissing my ears and neck and mouth, and saying how happy she was that she waited for the perfect man. She said it over and over and over.

Wow! I felt 10 feet tall. As simple as her words were, she couldn't have said anything in the world to make me feel better.

(5) In your opinion, what is the secret to being a seasoned, sensual senior, and what is one story you would like to tell that would help people understand how special sex can be to people over 60?

I thought I knew everything when I was younger, but the older I get, and I'm 69 now, the more I realize that I didn't really know a lot about anything before I met Genevieve. If I know anything at all about being a seasoned, sensual senior, as you call it, it's this: Real, true sexiness means being a diehard romantic, even when things don't work out like you think they should.

Now, that might sound funny from a crotchety old, white-haired, retired truck driver, but the one thing that my relationship with Genevieve has helped me learn that I really can be passionate without worrying about someone taking it away.

Thankfully, I do have Genevieve to return the passion. She is gone for a week right now to teach at a woman's retreat, which is why I'm here at this spa[2*] learning about getting healthier and developing better fitness and eating habits so we can enjoy a long, happy, healthy life together.

Being away from her makes me really miss her and the passion we have together. I really feel that God placed us together. And He has also prepared us to be able to grow together.

Like I've said before, Genevieve has really grown. I'm sure it has taken a lot of trust

---

2 * EDITOR'S NOTE: The resort mentioned in this chapter is very prestigious and expensive, maintains rigorous application standards, has an extensive waiting list of clients and does little commercial advertising; therefore, the resort owner has respectfully requested that we avoid mentioning the name of the resort for all the obvious reasons. Since a selected number of interviews for the Seasoned Romance™ Book Series have been conducted at this resort, we have agreed, of course, to honor that request.

on her part, since she had never been with a man before. She has learned to be very good in bed. She wasn't really sure whether she should do anything at first, and it took a lot of encouragement during the first few weeks to help her understand that I really liked her to take a very active role.

Before long, she was not only moving with me during intercourse, but she started initiating lots of things, too. She was kind of shy, which was so tender and wonderful, but I could that she really wanted to please me despite her lack of experience.

I can't tell you how great it is to say this, because it's something you would have to experience to understand, but it's like she is discovering for the first time what it's like to feel sexual as a woman. At the same time, she looks at me as if I were the only man in the world.

Just like I thought I had invented ejaculations when I was 14 and on the farm, it's almost like that as she discovers the glories of sex. Needless to say, I'm more than happy to be a willing partner in that ongoing discovery.

She is like an explorer, touching me everywhere, looking so closely at me. The other day, we spent at least an hour after taking a shower together, still completely naked, with me sitting on the edge of the bed, as she felt me all over and looked at my private parts, asking me dozens of questions.

Every time I make love to her, it's almost as if it's yet another first time for her. She gasps when I put my hand on her most sensitive areas. She murmurs and moans all the time when I suck on her nipples. Everything is so new to her. It seems like I can do no wrong.

Can you imagine what that does to a man's confidence and self-image? I can hardly believe that it's happening to me.

I just love it when we try a new position during intercourse. It's like she is a young woman with a whole new world opening up to her. And she loves it when I use feathers and other playful toys.

You wanted a specific example of how special sex can be. Let me talk about the night last weekend before she left for the women's retreat and I headed for this spa resort.

She made an incredible meal—roast duck, which is one of my favorites—and she placed it so beautifully on our dining room table, complete with all the serving dishes and a zillion forks and spoons. She doesn't drink alcohol, but she poured me a couple fingers of bourbon and brought it to me. After the meal, even though she doesn't like my cigars all that much, she opened up my humidor, brought me a cigar and lit it for me.

Then as I felt like a million bucks, satisfied from the wonderful gourmet food, sipping bourbon and taking puffs from the best-tasting cigar in the world, she sat on the opposite side of the table and simply looked so happy and beautiful that I thought my heart would explode from all the feelings I felt.

I don't know what made me do it, but I put the bourbon and cigar down, crawled under the table and stuck my head up between her legs. We do a lot of spontaneous, kid-like things, but that was pretty outrageous, I'll admit.

I did it just as a joke, but she wasn't expecting it. She couldn't see under the tablecloth, so she thought I had dropped something and was looking for it. When I touched her inner thighs so unexpectedly, she screamed and kicked the hell out of my stomach.

Of course, she quickly realized that I was just playing around and got down on her knees to kiss and apologize.

The kick had taken me by surprise, so I was gasping for air and couldn't explain what I had done. When I finally got my breath back, I still couldn't talk since both of us were laughing so hard. It might seem funny, but at that moment, with my stomach still smarting from her swift kick, I realized how much real love I felt for that woman.

What I'm saying is that the situation didn't start out being sexual, but it got that way very quickly. She kept kissing me, all over my stomach, still laughing and apologizing.

"I'm sorry, Honey, but you scared me when you touched me down there!" she finally said, trying to act like she was the wronged party.

"You kicked me," I yelled back, "so we're even." I realized then that I couldn't be mad at her even if I wanted to.

Obviously she felt what I was sensing. All of a sudden she kissed me and said, "Make love to me, Hal. Now. Here."

"Here?" I asked. "Under the table?"

"Why not?" she shot back. And right there, she completely took over. She actually screamed out loud when we came off together. That was the first time she had made so much noise, and that really set me off.

I realize that I've gone on and on, but it was the only way I knew to answer the question about how special sex can be at my age.

It's great! And she had better watch out when she gets back from the women's retreat. I've been planning things for her all week, and they involve some new toys I bought on the Internet! I am going to spend the rest of my years trying to make her happy.

Call me a hopeless romantic, but I'd rather be that with a life filled with passion than a shriveled up old guy with a dried-up dick.

A shriveled up old guy—it's interesting that I just used that phrase. That's what I probably would have become, and that's why I thank God everyday for bringing Genevieve into my life!

CECIL & ANNIE (BOTH 70)
EBONY & IVORY

"We are still together because we know we've got such a great thing going. I honestly think I would do almost anything for this man because he is always trying to come up with something new to delight and surprise me."

—ANNIE

(1) What is your age, background and general health?

ANNIE

Cecil and I are both 70 years old. We met when we were 60, ironically enough, at a funeral home while each of us was making arrangements for the funerals of our spouses. I was with some of my family members, all of us totally distraught. As we passed in the hallway, Cecil was with some of his family, obviously overcome with grief.

We're from a relatively small town, so we had seen each other at school events. Our children had been in the same school band and played on the same sports teams. We didn't run in the same social circles or anything. Plus, I am African-American, and he is White, and even in the so-called New South, sometimes there is still an invisible wall between us—sometimes the fault of both races, and often just because it is easier that way.

Anyway, as we passed in the hallway, I stopped and offered my condolences to him for the loss of his wife Betty, whom I had known fairly well. He tried to do the same thing for me, since I had just lost my husband

Jerome, who had been in a couple of civic organizations with Cecil.

It was one of those tense, uncomfortable moments when nothing you say really gets heard, and when everyone seems to be incredibly vulnerable. I guess it was definitely a sign that we are part of the New South, for Cecil and I suddenly hugged each other. It was one of those times when we simply forget the color of each other's skin and just tried to share our grief for a brief moment.

In retrospect, it might have looked somewhat strange to someone who just walked into the hall and saw the sight. Here were several of my Black family members on one side of the hall, and several White family members on the other side of the hall, and this short White guy and this taller Black woman hugging each other.

Anyway, we just held each other for a moment, then wished each other well and went on our separate ways. Nobody from either family said anything—I don't know if everyone was too grief-stricken or embarrassed by what the "old folk" were doing.

During the next month, I got through Jerome's funeral and legal affairs and all, and I ran into Cecil again at a grief support group at a church in our town. Before the evening was over, I had a whole new appreciation for him. Here was a guy, except for his mostly-bald head and some lines on his face, who looked like he could still play linebacker for a professional football team, which I found out he had done for a couple of seasons during his younger days. He was built like a bull with a big neck, shoulders and thighs, yet with a trim waist. Despite his tough guy appearance, he seemed willing to talk openly in the support group about the grief he was going through since his Betty died.

After the support group was over, I talked with Cecil for a few moments. He thanked me for being so sympathetic and understanding when we met in the hall at the funeral home. We hugged again briefly, then said goodbye to each other.

The next week, after the support group, we went out afterwards for coffee at a local restaurant. He was very easy to talk to, and I ended up unburdening a lot about myself on him. My marriage to Jerome had never been easy. He was a good man, but he had been very hurt by his parent's dysfunctional marriage, and he was never able to give very much of himself to me. Sexually, he was okay, but never very demonstrative toward me. I think he was afraid that if he let himself love me too much, I might reject him. Nothing could have been farther from the truth. It was hard for me to understand, since I had come from a family that was openly demonstrative and loving.

I tried and tried to get close to my first husband, but he always kept me at an arm's length. Unfortunately, he did the same thing with our five children. They were all good students, several were fine athletes, and all five went through college and now have good careers and wonderful families. Still, none of our children seemed to be able to do anything that was ever quite good enough for him. He was pretty critical, and hardly ever willing to offer praise. Again, I think the children and I all understood why he was what he was, but it didn't always make things easier to cope with.

I did my best to love that man, but I could hardly bring myself to cry for him when he was gone. In fact, there weren't a lot of tears shed for him at his funeral. My children and I loved him, but, silently, none of us liked him very much. He provided for us a nice living as a mechanic, but he just never could bring himself to return our love very well. And the saddest part was the discovery, after he was gone, that he had several long-term affairs in a nearby town that my children or myself knew nothing about. It was like getting kicked in the stomach when I found it out.

I can hardly talk about it now—even after all these years.

Cecil's story was exactly the opposite. He and Betty were hopelessly devoted to each other. They ran a commercial construction business, one of the largest in our area. His children and grandchildren were crazy about both Cecil and Betty. When she died quite unexpectedly, all of them were completely devastated.

Cecil and I spent many nights after the support group drinking decaffeinated coffee and talking. Nothing more. I guess we were quite a picture of contrasts—a short, White, balding ex-football player who liked country music, sitting with a tall, thin, Black grandmother who liked Big Band and Rhythm and Blues. But we also had a lot of similarities. We both had strong religious beliefs. We enjoyed card games and Western movies. We both dearly loved our children and grandchildren. And we both loved to travel, especially to the beach and the mountains.

Through the next weeks and months, I really grew to like him. I don't think either of us expected or anticipated anything deeper from the friendship, but I especially liked the fact that I felt so at ease with him, despite our cultural differences. Other than social acquaintances, I had never been all that close to a White before, and even though he had played on college and professional teams with Blacks through the years, he had never been particularly close to any of his African-American teammates.

I liked the fact that he didn't try to get too close or push me into anything more with him. I was very vulnerable with him, especially after I found out about my husband's affairs, and he could have used my exposed feelings to his advantage. Other men might have, but he didn't. He was the perfect gentleman, then and now. My respect grew immensely for him as I understood him better.

CECIL

I really liked Annie from the first time we started hanging out after the grief support meetings. I had known her and Jerome before, but we weren't close.

Annie was witty and had such a giving spirit, despite some of the hurts she had experienced.

She didn't know it, and I never made a major point about it, but I had grown up around some people that were pretty racist. I would like to think that it wasn't that way with me, but it probably rubbed off on me more than I thought. I played against Blacks in high school and got along with them well, and I was on the same teams with quite a few Blacks while I was in college and as a professional, but it's not like any of us were best buddies. It wasn't a conscious thing, but it just seemed to happen that way.

I remember a few times when I stood up for some of the Black players on my team, and they let me know that they appreciated it. Some of my White friends thought it was grandstanding, but I had simply been raised to treat all people with respect. They could have been purple or polka dot, for all I cared. It was the principle of the thing.

On the teams, I found that the Blacks pretty much stayed to themselves, and the Whites did the same. It wasn't antagonistic or anything, but just the way things went. We lived in different parts of town and stayed in different rooms in the hotels when we were on the road. It was a few years later that both Whites and Blacks started being more pro-active and even militant about breaking down barriers.

Staying in my own world wasn't an overt racial thing with me. We joked around and got along okay. I certainly didn't hate Blacks or anything, and I would have knocked anyone down that called me racist. I just didn't hang around with them much, and it was a pattern that continued through most of my adult life.

I played football professionally for a couple of years until my knees got blown out. At the same time it seemed like my daddy needed me at home with the construction business worse than my coaches did, especially with my bum knees. You didn't make a lot of money back then in football unless you were a star (and even then it was pennies compared to today's big money), so coming home to a regular paycheck without getting busted up in practice or games started looking more and more attractive.

I hired a lot of Blacks as laborers with my construction business, and some I promoted to be foremen and officers with the company, but again I don't want to take credit for being some kind of champion for racial equality or anything. I just always believed in hiring and promoting the best person for the job. Color of skin just never seemed all that important to me.

Still, as when I played football, I stayed in my own world and they lived in theirs. We would work alongside each other, and sometimes grab a meal or drinks together, but then we'd go our own way. Different social circles. Different churches. Just the way it was.

I've gone on and on about this, I know, but it helps explain why it was so unusual when Annie and I got together.

When Annie and I hugged in the funeral home, it wasn't something that I expected. It was as if we really reached past some walls as we embraced in the hallway.

After awhile, I couldn't wait to get with her the next time, and I could tell she felt the same way about me. It scared the hell out of me to have those feelings, and I think it did her, too. I guess that really does sound racist on both of our parts, doesn't it? Truth is, there was a lot more to it than skin color.

Anyway, even after I started realizing that there was more going on between us than just a simple friendship, I had to work through a lot of feelings. I wasn't sure. I mean, if we went deeper with our relationship, would she or I either be able to handle the racial difference? What would other people think? Our kids and grandkids?

This was the New South and all, but we were both products of the Old South. Both of us had grown up in very different worlds, even though we only lived a few miles apart.

Finally, I simply decided to make a move and find out if we had a chance. I invited her to church with me for a special music program. She came with me, and everyone greeted her warmly and accepted the fact that we were together.

Then we went on a date, dancing to the Big Band music she loved so much and a candlelight dinner. Dancing was a hoot—me with my busted up ole knees and her gracefully trying to stay out of the way of my two left feet, smiling as if she were dancing with Fred Astaire or Gregory Hines.

People in the town may have talked about us. In fact, I'm sure they did. But no one seemed to care that we were together. In fact, since most knew about our similar losses, I think people were genuinely happy for us.

I invited her out to drive around to some of my construction sites, and all my workers tipped their hardhats and went on about their business without staring or anything. Frankly, it was no big deal to them, I suppose. It was more of a potential stumbling block to us.

I mean, we were quite a sight. She said I'm built like a bull. If that's true, she's built like fine china. I'm tanned, but still very White. She is very dark-skinned. No one seemed to care about our differences. If they did, they didn't say anything.

Then we took the ultimate challenge. We invited her family and my family all over to my house for a big Fourth of July picnic.

I honestly didn't know how everyone would react, but I figured that we needed to know if anyone had problems with the two of us being together.

If I wondered, I shouldn't have. The little kids took over and within a few minutes of arriving, there were little Black grandkids and little White grandkids playing games together. Most of them knew each other from school. Some even worked together.

In fact, most of my kids and her kids had gone to grade school, middle school, high school and even the same colleges together. Some had been on the same sports teams, cheerleading squads and marching bands, so within minutes they were talking and laughing about all the memories.

I saw members of both families playing on the basketball court together, and others swimming in the pool together. Frankly, any thought about color differences was simply no big deal to them. The fact that I thought it might be showed that I had worried about nothing.

That night, as we sat beside the lake at the back of my property and watched the town's fireworks celebration, I slipped my arm around Annie's trim waist and stood there barely able to contain my happiness. She smiled at me, circled her arm around my waist and leaned her head softly against mine.

In the semi-darkness, I heard one of my grandsons tell one of her grandsons, "Lookee there at my Paw-paw and your Grammie." It was during a sudden lull in the fireworks, so everyone around heard the words. I heard some overly-dramatic "ooohs" and "ahhhs," but everyone seemed to take it all in stride.

That night, as all the kids and grandkids were leaving, laden down with leftover barbecue and desserts, every one of our children—hers and mine—let us know, in their own way, that they were happy for us and approved of what we were doing. One of her kids even joked about us being "Ebony and Ivory," like the Stevie Wonder and Paul McCartney song back in the Eighties. I guess it described us pretty well.

Later that night, we walked all alone back out to the dock beside the lake. I took her in my arms and held her for a long time without either of us saying a word. Then I kissed her for the first time. Then we kissed again and again.

Neither of us had ever pushed the romantic part of our relationship until then. Maybe we had too much to work through in all the other areas of our lives. But at that moment, there was no doubt, physically or otherwise, that something was happening in a very warm, sensual way. We both realized that we were tearing down one of the last walls between us. And when we knocked it down, the feelings came rushing over us like a flood.

We didn't go over the line sexually that night, but we came pretty close. We were like magnets being drawn together, and the lustiness of our kisses spread like wildfire. Finally, we pulled apart and I walked her through the yard, past the pool and basketball court, and out to her car.

ANNIE

He was always the perfect gentleman, even that first night that we kissed. Both of us, though we hadn't discussed it, had always taught our children the importance of getting married before having sex and being committed to one women-one man during marriage.

As the heat grew between us that night on the pier, I knew I couldn't go through with making love, but I also was afraid that I couldn't stop. It was very powerful between us, like something bigger than us had taken over. I was on fire inside, and I was pretty sure he was, too.

Thankfully, he did stop before we went too far, and my admiration and respect grew for him immeasurably, although I must admit that my body was begging for him to get on with it.

What we both knew, as we discussed later that night, was that we had to either cool things off or go ahead and get married. Once we reached that point of actually talking about marriage, neither of us was willing to cool it too long, so we made plans to go ahead with a small family-members-only wedding in two weeks. Those were the longest two weeks for both of us. Some of our friends thought we were going too fast and should wait until at least a year after our spouses passed away before getting married. Even to this day, I never understood logic like that, even though I would have probably given the same advice to a friend in a similar situation. We were deeply, over-the-edge in love, and we felt a real peace about what we were doing. A few friends told us that it wouldn't last, not because of the color difference, but because we were jumping into marriage before dating others and making sure of what we wanted in life.

We already knew. We wanted each other. Oh, how we wanted each other! I ached for him, maybe because it had been so long since I felt those feelings.

After the wedding was over, we said our goodbyes to our family members, then jumped in his car and headed for a resort less than an hour away from our home. I could hardly stand the hour's wait. I really wanted him. I had never had sex with a White man before, nor with anyone besides Jerome before or during our marriage, and we had seldom had sex at all during the last 10 years of Jerome's life because he was increasingly ill.

I was like a rambunctious teenager, so excited at being in bed with Cecil that it was all I could do to keep from ripping off his pants in the car as we drove. I tried to be coy, touching him on the leg and squeezing his arm as we talked and drove, but my mind was racing with hopes that he was as good in bed as he was good in every other area of his life.

When we got in the room, he asked if I wanted to order dinner, go for a swim or...? I didn't even give him a chance to finish his question. Maybe I shocked him a little, but he seemed very pleased when I told him "I want your tight White ass in bed right now!" We both laughed, for it really wasn't the kind of language I normally used, but it seemed appropriate at the moment.

I went into the bathroom and dressed in lingerie I had bought for our honeymoon. When I came out from the bathroom, he was sitting on the edge of the bed with a beautifully-wrapped gift sitting in his lap.

When I got on the bed beside him, he held the gift out to me. Inside was the most beautiful white diamond and black pearl bracelet I had ever seen.

"It's for you," he said very tenderly. "You're my black pearl, and my love for you is as eternal as these diamonds." I melted! Literally. If I had ever doubted that I was doing the right thing by marrying Cecil, I knew at that moment that God had given me an extraordinary man to have and hold. Even if he had been a dud in bed, I knew I had gotten the deal of the century by being in love with him.

Thankfully, he was hardly a dud. He was as warm and thoughtful and wonderful as I'd hoped. He was a giver, not just a taker. I never knew what it was like to be with a man like that before. He was infinitely more interested in what I wanted than what he wanted.

I must admit that my eyes kept going down toward his midsection. I had never seen a White man's "Willie" before, not that it looked all that different from a Black man's except for the color, of course.

He was in no hurry for awhile, taking his time to explore everything. He probably had never seen a Black woman this closely before, and he seemed amazed at how I was dark almost everywhere.

In fact, while we were making love, I happened to look at the big closet mirrors at the end of our bed. I could see our buttocks, and—best of all—I could see the stark contrast of his White maleness, shimmering with my liquid, going deep inside my Blackness, sliding in, then sliding out. Seeing that sight sent shockwaves deep inside me. It was such an unexpected emotion, and I was unprepared for how absolutely sensual it was to see our contrasting skin pulling and pushing together.

When the pace picked up, it really started jumping. My fire had been lit for weeks, and I needed his "Willie" to quench that fire. When Cecil finally blew his top inside me, I literally passed out for a moment. I had never done that before, and it scared me to death.

It wasn't the last time I passed out, and it wasn't the last time I woke up with a start after only a moment of unconsciousness to see him over me.

It was, however, the moment that I realized that I was on an odyssey with a man who had made me feel like more of a woman than ever before, who was totally interested in making me feel satisfied.

Sometimes with Jerome I had wondered whether there was something wrong with me, since he didn't seem to get much past the "Wham-bam-thank-you-ma'am" part. I often questioned whether I was some sort of pervert because I couldn't wait for Jerome to go to bed so I could slip into the bathroom and touch myself until I reached an orgasm. Not once did Jerome get me over the top—not once in all the years we were married. I tried to get him to, but he seemed to think it was my problem.

With Cecil, there was no problem. He enjoyed doing anything he could to help put me over the top. And, boy, was I happy to go on that delicious journey with him! I felt like a young newlywed, just learning how good it could feel deep inside.

That night as we fell asleep in each other's arms, the last thought that ran through my mind was that I couldn't wait to do it again, and again, and again. I was a woman in love, and for the first time in my life, I had a man who loved me back as much as I loved him.

And I fell asleep with the vivid image of his White sexual parts, shiny and wet, going inside my Blackness. I almost woke him up to see if he would do it again, but I restrained myself.

You see, unless you have lived in a marriage without that kind of love and love-making, there is no way of knowing how wonderful it feels to have someone like Cecil in your life.

(2) Is sex still a part of your life, and, if so, how has it (and you) changed over the years?

CECIL

Sex was always a part of my life. I always enjoyed sex, and Betty and I had it regularly. It tapered off some as we got into our middle years, especially as the family and business responsibilities kept adding up.

I really missed making love after Betty passed away. Making love has always been more than having sex, and it was the closeness that I really missed. Being with Annie has been really good, because I have got to feel that closeness again. We have gotten increasingly familiar and more willing to cut up more, having fun together, as the years have gone on with Annie and me.

ANNIE

Without belaboring the point, sex with Jerome was more of a time of pain for me than anything, not physical pain, but the pain of wondering why I wasn't able to reach him and get him to open up to me. Don't get me wrong. I loved Jerome and cherish the years we spent together, but it is so different now. I am more secure and know that much, if not all, of the problem was with him, not just with me as I felt all those years.

Sex with Cecil is a never ending adventure. He is always coming up with something new, some way to express himself better or some new shenanigan he is up to. He says that he likes to keep it fresh and alive, and I believe him. That man is crazy at times, always keeps me in stitches, and I'm crazy about him.

(3) If you are currently involved in an intimate relationship, how long has it lasted? What has made it last? What have been the best (or worse) parts of the relationship?

ANNIE

We are still together because we know we've got such a great thing going. I honestly think I would do almost anything for this man because he is always trying to come up with something new to delight and surprise me.

(4) What details about you, your partner and your relationship would surprise people if they knew?

CECIL

I think the thing that might surprise others about us is that we hardly ever think about her being Black and me being White anymore. Truly. I hardly ever think about it, except when she gets around some of her lady friends and they start talking real fast about "Girl this" and "Girl that." Once in awhile someone sees us together and does a double-take when they find out that we are married, but we don't let it bother us. Why should we?

Actually, the thing that would probably surprise people most about us, if they knew, is that we like to surprise each other, often in sexual ways. I'm always trying to do something that will make her enjoy our lovemaking more.

I've started writing love poems, which is something I never did before. If my college writing professors knew I was doing that, they'd roll over in their grave! I barely made it through bone-head English, and only did that because my coach was threatening the teacher if his star linebacker didn't pass her class. But now I've started writing things for her, little poems and notes. She either likes them a lot or is a darn good actress.

Part of the way we surprise each other is by coming up with unusual ways to make love. I'm not talking about real strange or kinky things, but good ones. One time we were looking at an old movie, and she talked about how much she used to love the Superman movies. I went out the next day to a costume shop and got ready for the next time we made love. When she went into the bathroom before we got started, I got a full-blown Superman suit on, right down to the cape, put on a black shiny wig, and got underneath the covers. When she came out of the bathroom and walked over to the bed, she laughed and asked me what I was doing underneath the covers. I threw back the covers, jumped up on my feet and ran around the room, acting like I was flying. She shrieked with laughter. Actually, we never did make love that evening. We kept laughing too hard at my get-up and wig.

Another time, just recently, we were in San Diego for a long weekend and spent an afternoon at the famous zoo there. Wouldn't you know it, when we were standing with a crowd in front of the lion's area, which was her favorite animal, by the way, one of the big male lions decided to give it to one of the female lions. Neither of us had ever seen lions make it before. Obviously, judging from all the snickering and eyes bugging out, few of the others had seen it happen before. There was some major hip action, snarling and roaring in the lions' habitat, but it was over pretty quick, and everything went back to normal.

On the cab drive back to our hotel, Annie started touching my "Willie," as she calls it. I was embarrassed, since we were in a cab, but she was really into it and the cabbie had no idea what we were doing. Thankfully, we got to the hotel fairly quick, and when we got back to the room, she told me how hot it had made her to watch the big male lion stick it to the female lion, especially when he did the hard thrusts with all the roaring, and to see how much in heat the female lion was.

She told me again how much she had always liked lions, anyway, and how sexy she thought it was that we had seen them do it. Then she rolled over, got on her knees, and asked me to do it from the back like the lions.

I love doing it that way. I don't exactly know why. I think it's simply the angle that feels so good. I had started to initiate it a time or two with Annie, but she never wanted to do it that way because her first husband sometimes did it to her when he was drunk and wasn't willing to use any lubrication or to wait for her to get ready. It had always hurt her before with Jerome, so I let it drop and didn't push the issue.

Well, after we saw the lions, she let me know that she wanted to do it from the back. She certainly didn't need any extra lubrication, that was evident when I touched her to see if she was ready. Her panties were soaked. That was a powerful aphrodisiac for me. I didn't care if it was a little kinky for her to be fantasizing about lions humping.

When I approached her from the back and went inside her, she started making lioness-type noises. That was exciting for me, and I decided to get into it, too, pretending to roar like a big lion as I slid into her and started giving her strokes.

Wow! When I roared, she started hunching and gasping. Well, I may not be the smartest guy in the world, but I didn't need any more of a hint to keep roaring and thrusting. Then she fell limp on the bed. I came out of her as she fell, so I was standing over her, trying to turn her over and see if she was okay when she blinked her eyes. I had heard of women who have such intense orgasms that they pass out for a second or so, but I didn't know if it was really true until I saw it happen to Annie. It scared the hell out of me at first. I thought I'd killed her or something.

Anyway, she quickly came roaring back to life and wanted more from the back. She didn't have to ask twice. Thankfully, she didn't pass out again, but she had another orgasm before I went off.

I mentioned before that there's something really intense to me when I do it to her from the back—something about the pressure it puts on the bottom of my penis head. I roared a lot that afternoon when I came, but I wasn't just trying to act like a male lion. For a little while, I really WAS the king of our personal jungle!

But that's not the end of the lion story. Not by a long shot. Hopefully you won't laugh too much as I tell this.

Annie is a pretty good seamstress, especially since she spent most of her young life working on a sewing machine in a mill, and one day she decided to make me a costume. She didn't tell me about it until it was all made, and one evening after we had been swimming nude in our pool, then took a dip in the hot tub, it was pretty evident that "Willie" wanted to take a dip, too.

We came into the bedroom, and she had me stand by the bed "for a little surprise." She went to the stereo, popped in a CD, and hit the switch. She had gone to one of the wilderness-type stores at a mall and got a CD of lions roaring and mating. At least it sounded like they were mating, but they could have been fighting for all I knew. I liked it. I had enjoyed playing "lion" before and the CD sounds only added to the great feeling welling up inside me.

Then she told me to close my eyes and headed for her closet. When she told me to open my eyes, she was holding a full-length lion's costume, right down to the eyes, teeth, mane and tail! I couldn't believe how good she had done. She helped me put it on and zipped me up. Since my penis was stiff, I was a bit concerned about zipping it in. Not to worry! She had built a "Willie" flap, as she called it, so I was completely unrestricted and ready for action.

She was really getting into it, and so was I. All the mating sounds and heavy breathing from the stereo made me even more excited. It was hot inside the costume, so I wanted to get in on as soon as possible and get out.

She decided to do it from the front, lying on her back, so she could see me in my costume better.

At that point, I would have been willing to do it hanging by one foot from the ceiling! The lion's sounds on the CD were getting to me in a big way.

Again, she needed no lubrication. As I started giving it to her, she kept telling me how great it felt with all the rough material rubbing all over her. I could tell that both of us were going to blow our tops very quickly, so I gave her some fast strokes as fast as I could. I started coming first. I roared as loud as I could and kept stroking real fast.

Sure enough, when she reached her peak she fell limp like she had done before when we played "lion" previously, only this time I was on top and could keep giving her strokes as I unloaded inside her.

She was only out for a moment, and when she opened her eyes, she jerked away from me and began screaming in fear. Only then did I remember the lion's suit. It took her a moment to figure out what was going on and why a lion was pumping it into her!

Then she started laughing. And then I fell on the floor laughing.

And if that wasn't funny enough, the phone rang and our next door neighbor, who lives several hundred feet and an eight-foot privacy fence away, was wanting to make sure that everything was okay. He had heard a bunch of loud noises and wanted to see if we had, too! I guess we had the stereo volume turned up pretty loud after all, and our own roaring noises only added to the volume that bothered our neighbor.

Yeah, I guess for a couple of old White and Black grandparents, we do some things that might surprise a few people. But it's all done in fun, and we're enjoying sex and being together more than either of us ever dreamed possible.

(5) In your opinion, what is the secret to being a seasoned, sensual senior, and what is one story you would like to tell that would help people understand how special sex can be to people over 60?

CECIL

Instead of talking about us, let me tell you about our neighbor, Clyde, who is almost 90 and his wife, Hannah, is 85. They are good people, pretty well off and seem to have a good marriage that has lasted since they were teenagers. Most of that time, at least until the past 15 years or so that I've known them, they had a big ranching operation 30 miles or so from our town. Since I built my house beside theirs, we've become good friends. When I lost Betty, they sort of took me under their wing—the son they never had, I suppose. I try to check on them at least once a day. Betty used to bake and cook things for them, and Annie has done the same thing.

Anyway, I went over one day to check on them and give them a loaf of Annie's freshly-baked bread. Clyde always likes it when I come over and sit and jaw with him. He's a diehard country music fan like me, so he always has some old Ferlin Husky, Wilburn Brothers or Loretta Lynn songs on his stereo and listens to it through a speaker system I installed for him out on his porch.

You don't have to be around them long to see how much Clyde and Hannah love each other. Sometimes I look over and see them dancing on the porch with the country music playing. Both of them are still pretty spry and they dance the two-step like they were in their thirties.

Clyde is always cutting up and making some reference to doing it with Hannah. Anytime I bring a loaf of bread over, he invariably brings "puttin' his loaf in Hannah's oven" somewhere in the conversation. When I bring over a pie or cake, he will somehow talk about "gettin' some of Hannah's sugar." He's just a really good old guy, but he embarrasses the hell out of Hannah when he jokes around that way.

He doesn't do it in some sick or perverted way. It's actually pretty touching to see the old folks when they seem to be getting a little frisky.

Anyway, Clyde and I sat out there for awhile as his wife Hannah went back in the house to make some coffee to go with the bread. He asked me about the roaring noises again, and I decided to tell him the truth, or at least what I thought he could handle. He laughed and cackled until I thought he would fall over. When he would stop laughing, I'd roar like a lion and we'd both start laughing again.

Then he did the damnedest thing. He grinned real big, made a circle out of his left forefinger and thumb, stuck his right forefinger into the circle, poked it in and out a couple of times, then gestured toward the kitchen where his wife was making coffee.

"Run back over to your house and get that damned lion CD," he said slyly. "I've got a hankering to give her a good poking, and she's just loves lions in the movies and those animal shows. Who knows? It may work wonders for getting some of Hannah's sugar."

I didn't know if Clyde was joking or not, but I beat a path back to my house and retrieved the CD. Hannah and him were sitting on the porch holding hands when I came back, so I quickly handed him the CD, winked and told them I needed to head back to get some chores done.

Oh, and by the way, the damned old fool neighbor of mine still hasn't given me the CD back. I downloaded it on my computer so I could make more CDs, so I don't really need the CD back, but I keep bringing it up, joking with the old codger about needing it back really bad, telling him that he's getting all the action since I don't have the CD anymore. He just cackles.

When I go over, he sometimes roars like a lion a time or two, his wife gets red-faced and heads inside to get coffee for us, and we have a good laugh.

I act real serious-like and say that I really need that CD back. If his wife isn't around, he makes that same motion with one forefinger giving it to a circle of his other forefinger and thumb, then gestures toward wherever his wife is and grins real big and says the same thing every time: "Boy, you'd better leave that CD with me a little bit longer. Hannah loves them damned lions, and I love Hannah when she gets hawg wild. She's turned into this flirty thing, and there ain't been this much pokin' going on around here for 40 years. Hannah's about to wear this ole guy out!"

Like I said before, I guess you never get too old.

If Clyde is lying to me, I don't want to know. It's too much fun thinking that when I turn 90 Ebony and Ivory will still be "pokin' it." I sure hope so!

GUENTHER (81)
TWICE AS GOOD

"Every summer we used to go to a mountain lodge in Canada for a week. It was pretty desolate, and we were usually all by ourselves, so we did it more than usual, and she seemed invigorated by the surroundings. She was from a Norwegian background and

I am mostly German, neither of which is known for being diehard romantics, but we did okay for ourselves when the fever hit."
—GUENTHER

(1) What is your age, background and general health?

I am 81 years old. Most of my life I ran several banks in the Midwest, a company started by my father. I was married to a wonderful woman named Margaret from the time we were 20 until she died 10 years ago. Sometimes I called her Margo or Margie, so if I call her that while we talk today, you'll understand that they were all the same names for my wife.

We lived in the same town as my twin brother Gus and his wife Sonja. Most people couldn't tell us apart, except I almost always wore a suit and tie, while Gus, who ran an insurance company, often wore a sweater. Even our parents could hardly tell us apart, and certainly not our schoolteachers or college professors.

Actually, Margaret sometimes said that both Gus and I looked like identical Ichabod Cranes! She didn't mean it negatively, but it really was true. Both of us were always a bit too thin, too bony, too bossy, too intense and too scowling. Our hair, especially mine, never quite combed right. It only got worse as both of our heads turned pure white. We were both nice looking and dressed well, but we weren't handsome, in any classic sense. We just looked hardhearted, I suppose, because both of us were in professions where we had to deal with people who were sometimes hurt, scared, desperate, or worse—those trying to run a ruse.

We really weren't crotchety old men. That wasn't the way we really were deep inside. We both liked to joke around and have a good time when out of the public eye, but out in the communities where we worked, I guess we always felt as if we had to be professional and distant. Pictures of us do look pretty grim. Our father was like that too, so maybe that's where we got it.

Sonja died almost 10 years before Margaret died, and Gus passed away not long after Margo. My wife and I didn't have any little ones, but Gus and Sonja had four, and we loved all their kids like our own. They now have families who have families, and the kids and grandkids live all over the place.

As for health, I could be better, but I'm not bad for an 81 year old man. I've gone through heart bypass operations two times. I take a few medicines. I take trips sometimes, and I stay pretty active. I still walk a couple of miles nearly every day through the park near my home, and I spend a few months each winter at a home I bought a couple of years ago down in South Texas. I also go two spas each year for at least a week.[3*]

(2) Is sex still a part of your life, and, if so, how has it (and you) changed over the years?

Sex was always a part of my life. Margaret and I didn't exactly set the woods on fire all the time, I suppose, but we did okay. I was always pretty busy with the banks, especially during times when farmers and businesses all over the area were in trouble—which seemed like

---

3 * EDITOR'S NOTE: Both of the resorts mentioned in this chapter are very prestigious and expensive, maintain rigorous application standards, have an extensive waiting list of clients and do little commercial advertising; therefore, the resort owners have respectfully requested that we avoid mentioning the names of these resorts for all the obvious reasons. Since a selected number of interviews for the Seasoned Romance™ Book Series have been conducted at both resorts, we have agreed, of course, to honor that request.

most of the time. Margie stayed busy with her sewing and quilting and church guild.

Neither of us knew a lot about sex when we got married, and what we learned, we learned together. As she got more comfortable talking about sex, she would tell me what she liked, and I got pretty good at satisfying her. Again, I was no handsome Don Juan, I suppose, but we got along well.

We always seemed to enjoy our best sex when we got away from home. She had always wanted children, and when we couldn't have any, it was pretty distressing to her. Getting away from our home and staying in a big, fine hotel always seemed to make her more interested in romance.

Every summer we used to go to a mountain lodge in Canada for a week. It was pretty desolate, and we were usually all by ourselves, so we did it more than usual, and she seemed invigorated by the surroundings. She was from a Norwegian background and I am mostly German, neither of which is known for being diehard romantics, but we did okay for ourselves when the fever hit.

As for sex being part of my life now, I can't say it is too much. Oh, I still act like a 14-year-old from time to time, playing with myself, imagining myself with Margaret or some other blonde Norwegian nymph. I often do it with my hands, but I've also got a couple of things I ordered through the mail—one called the Ooh-La-La® **(EDITOR'S NOTE: We were so impressed with Guenther's description that we researched this well-designed male-response tool, received more and more great testimonials from men of different ages from around the world, and have since made this excellent product available on the DeLeeuw Research Group's Website, www.FirePointe.com)** that vibrates on my dick head splendidly. I also ordered and occasionally use a couple of realistic-feeling, vagina-looking masturbators, and while they aren't quite the same as the real thing, I get by quite nicely when I want to.

But I have to be very careful being with women, sad to say. I'm one of the wealthiest men in my area, and sometimes I get the feeling that I can't always trust some of the gals who try to get close to this old guy, either at the banks or elsewhere in the communities where I am well known. So, mostly, I associate with trusted co-workers and a few close friends when I am around my home. I do take trips where I sometimes meet women who don't care whether I have money or not, but even then I am very careful.

In other words, I'd like to have more of a sex life, but I'm not going to risk my reputation or act the fool just to be with a woman. If it happens, it happens.

(3) If you are currently involved in an intimate relationship, how long has it lasted? What has made it last? What have been the best (or worse) parts of the relationship?

I'm not in an intimate relationship now. Other than on trips to Minneapolis and down in South Texas, I haven't gone on too many dates, and I have not had sex at all, other than self-pleasuring occasionally when the mood strikes me.

However, I really miss how good it feels to be with a caring, loving woman, to be inside her and knowing that you are giving her pleasure while receiving the most wonderful gift in return. I'd like to be in love again sometime, but I don't know if it will ever happen. Whether it does or not, I feel as if I've already had a pretty fine run for the roses.

(4) What details about you, your partner and your relationship would surprise people if they knew?

In all the years we were married, Margaret had one thing she did that really got to me. Even though she lived most of her life in America, her parents came directly from Norway, and they always talked in their mother tongue in the home. All the years I knew her, she could talk English fairly well, but she thought and dreamed in Norwegian all her life. She never lost that accent that I grew to love so well.

And when Margo and I made love, she always spoke in Norwegian when she got excited. It was kind of strange, at first, but I really grew to like it. As she got closer to a peak, she would begin talking Norwegian real fast and scratching my backside. It was the damnedest thing! By the time I shot inside her, she would be squealing all these funny words and clawing me with her fingernails. It got to the point that I had to wear my under-shirt when we had sex to keep my skinny backside in one piece. Sometimes even the undershirt didn't help much.

Funny thing is, though, I got to the point that I actually shot off because of her squeal-ing and clawing, not just because I was mov-ing up and down inside her. It was one of the things that I really liked about her.

As for details about something that would surprise people if they knew about us, I guess now is as good of a time to tell this as any. I'm not particularly proud of it, but I'm not really unhappy about it, either.

We were in our mid-sixties when Gus' wife Sonja died. My twin brother went to pieces for awhile. He sold his insurance business and most of his real estate, then traveled to see his kids and grandkids for awhile. They're scattered from here to California.

When he came back, he stayed in his house all by himself. He lived about five miles away from ours, so Margo and I would drive over from time to time to keep an eye on him. I really worried about him and felt sorry for him, since it was so obvious that he was grieving so deeply. He was as alone and lonely as anyone I had ever seen. He and Sonja had been very much in love, and he really missed her beyond any words that he could express.

He tried to act like he was the same old Gus, but it was like the life had gone out of his eyes. He lost weight. He's pretty skinny like me anyway, so he started looking pretty gaunt. He still took care of himself and you'd see him around town from time to time, but a lot of times I'd drive by to see him, and he'd be sitting in a darkened house. Just sitting there. It was like he had simply given up.

One night when he was coming over for dinner, I decided to ask Margaret if she would consider going to bed with him, just once, to let him see that life wasn't over and that he was still a spring chicken, so to speak. It seemed like the thing to do at the time, maybe the only thing I had that could get him past the grief he was feeling. Secretly, I hoped it would be the one thing that would snap him out of such deep depression and see that he could live again.

That sort of thing flew in the face of everything we believed, being strict Lutherans and all, but I really loved my brother, and I wanted him to be happy. I was ready to try almost anything. I didn't want to let my twin brother slip away without a fight.

The strangest thing is that Margie agreed. She had loved Gus most of her life, too, since he and Sonja had been so close all the years.

"It will be like making love with you," Margie said. "You and Gus are so much alike."

Maybe she liked the idea of seeing if twins did it differently or something, but I didn't care. I was willing to share her with him, since Margaret and Gus were the two people on the earth that I loved most.

Again, I just wanted to see my brother happy and vigorous again, like the Gus I had always known.

After he got to our house for dinner, we ate for awhile, then we went into the parlor where the fireplace was blazing. After a couple of brandies, I told him what I had in mind, and that Margaret was waiting for him in the bedroom. He looked surprised, of course, but after I encouraged him, he went in the bedroom with her and didn't come out for awhile.

I must say that it was one of the strangest experiences for me as I sat there by the fire. On the one hand, I didn't like the idea of my brother shooting off inside my wife of over 40 years.

I was genuinely glad that Gus and Margaret were doing it, and yet a part of me wasn't so sure. I was happy for him, yet I was a bit jealous for me. What if she liked him better?

On the other hand, even though the sounds were muffled, as I heard the bedsprings creaking and them breathing harder and harder, it made me so aroused I could barely stand it.

I heard him moan a few times, her squealing a little and then the noises stopped. In a few minutes he came out of the room. He looked so serious as he sat down beside me and sipped the rest of his brandy. I think he was trying to decide if he should say something about whether it was good or not. It's not the kind of thing that you normally talk about, even as twins, so neither of us said anything. Then he said, "I'd better run on home."

I walked him to the door. Right before he stepped outside, he turned around and said one word: "Thanks."

That was it. He was enough like me that it was all I expected. I saw the light in his eyes, and it spoke volumes.

After he backed his car out of the driveway and drove away, I went back inside. My gal Margie was waiting at our bedroom door. She motioned me toward her. When we entered the bedroom, she dropped her bathrobe, lay down, and patted the bed for me to join her.

"Was it okay with him?" I asked her. "Did he like it or . . ?"

"You brother felt good," she said, "but he went pretty quick. I like you best, and I want you to do it some more."

She seemed very excited at having both of us, one after the other. I must say it was very strange to look down at her pubic area, already juiced up. All the squealing Norwegian phrases were already coming out from the time I slid inside her.

I'm not sure I want to understand why it was so pleasurable. There's probably some deep psychological reason for it. I'm sure some psychiatrist could have a heyday with all the implications—Freudian, homosexual and otherwise. But I really don't care what others think, even now as I am telling it to you.

I guess only a twin could understand what I just said, and I'm not sure I do at all. I'm not even sure it has anything to do with being a twin, though I know that I never would have offered or even stood for Margaret to ever be with anyone else.

A few days later Gus and I met for lunch. It was the first time we had talked since he was with Margo. I wanted to feel guilty about what the three of us had done—upstanding citizens of the community and all—but I just couldn't. It was wrong, I suppose, but I didn't feel a bit bad about it.

Finally, Gus looked at me and said, "Guenther, you gave me one of the best gifts I've ever got. You're a good brother."

I didn't know what to say. Again, it's not the kind of thing that brothers normally talk about, so we sat in silence for awhile longer.

Finally, once again, Gus broke the silence.

"What the hell was Margaret talking about with all that Norwegian gibberish?" he asked.

I couldn't help joking with him. I tried to keep from smiling as I cracked, "She said Gus' little needle dick is okay, but Guenther's mighty prick is the best!"

Gus punched me in the arm like he used to when we were kids. He knew that we were both the same size, the mirror image in just about everything except a few scars and the way we combed our hair. He and I started snickering like teenagers, then we both roared with laughter with our sides hurting. Like I had hoped, Gus eyes were bright again. He was smiling.

Then he asked, "Does she always scratch the hell out of your back?" I told him that the next time he should keep his damn undershirt on.

The next time?

I couldn't believe I said that, but it seemed okay. If it meant seeing my brother happy again, I would share Margaret with him forever. He smiled.

Thankfully, Margo didn't seem to mind. In fact, I think she grew to enjoy having her two "Ichabod Cranes" vying for her attention. And so for the next 10 years, until Gus had a heart attack on a drive back from seeing kids in California, Margaret had two identical lovers, Gus and me. If she minded, she never said anything about it. Margie seemed to be having a good time, and Gus was happier than I had ever seen him.

We did it together a few times. By "together," I mean ALL three of us in the same bed, a *ménage à trios*, though it didn't include Gus and I actually touching or doing anything to each other. That would have been taking it too far for either of us. We just did it with her, one after the other, but it was really kind of exciting to see him poking her. We never talked about it, but I think he liked watching me poke it to her, too. Actually, it was usually Margaret's idea when all three of us got in bed together at the same time, so I know she liked it. She told me that she enjoyed lying between us, then all of us falling asleep together.

And of the most memorable times, I think of the time just one year before Margaret and Gus passed away that all three of us went up to our mountain lodge together. There wasn't the privacy of a bedroom, since it was like one big room, so we spent all the time together.

The lodge had a huge fireplace, so the embers made it even more romantic and memorable.

Gus and I made love to Margaret several times during the week. By this time, we were comfortable enough with the situation that it didn't seem to matter to any of us that what we were doing was kind of strange for three old Lutherans who should have known better.

One night Margaret came up with a game she invented and called "choo-choo train," or sometimes she'd sometimes call it *"jernbane tog,"* where Gus would go inside Margaret and hit a few strokes, then he would get out and back up while I would get in for a few strokes. Margaret enjoyed telling us when we had to switch. Thankfully she did it mostly in English. We went for awhile that night, laughing and playing "choo-choo." We even made train sounds when it was our time to get inside her.

Finally, I couldn't stand it anymore. Margie told me to switch, but I was too close to the edge and kept going as hard as I could. She yelled for me to switch again, but by then I was already shooting it off inside her. All of a sudden, she stopped yelling "Switch!" and started scratching and screaming a string of Norwegian words.

Gus was primed and ready, and see-ing him go off inside her with her squealing Norwegian was like looking at a mirror of me doing it. I liked watching his prick all shiny as it slid in and out. It was like getting to have sex and watch myself doing it, too, sort of like a mirror.

We all enjoyed *"jernbane tog"* and played it a number of times after that, doing it from both front and back. Margaret really liked doing it where she could yell "Switch!" She even played "choo-choo" with her mouth a few times when she was too sore down below from too much Guenther and Gus locomo-tion, I suppose.

But I don't want it to seem that we only had sex when the three of us were together. I remember the sex times best, but there were lots of other times that the three of us lay in bed as both Gus and I touched her and kissed her. Sometimes I couldn't keep from feeling a little jealous when they kissed in front of me, but she always made me feel great again when she turned to me and asked me to kiss her. Thankfully, she had plenty of love and tenderness for both of us.

I wouldn't recommend it for anyone else, and I suppose that the potential for disaster was there, but it all seemed to work real well for the three of us for nearly 10 memorable years. Maybe being twins made it easier, but I can't say, since I don't know if other twins would react the same way under different circumstances.

5. **In your opinion, what is the secret to being a seasoned, sensual senior, and what is one story you would like to tell that would help people understand how special sex can be to people over 60?**

I still feel very sexual, even now, but I don't know if I will ever feel like I did toward Margaret with someone else, especially after the 10 years with Gus when we all grew very, very close. I like to watch beautiful women walking along the beach when I am down in South Texas or at one of the spas where I go. Even in the frozen Northland, I can even get pretty worked up just looking at women walking past me in winter coats. I like feeling that way. It makes me feel alive.

I don't think I could do it with any woman, at the drop of a hat, but if I were in love with her and if the time was right, I could still do it. I'd probably feel guilty if I didn't get married first. But I could do it. After all, if I can still shoot some into the Ooh-La-La®, those pink-vagina-looking masturbators or even a tissue when I'm using my hands, even though what comes out is much less than in my prime, then I'm sure I could still do it inside a beautiful woman. I'd like to think so, at least. That thought often keeps me warm at night.

I know for a fact that life isn't over just because you turn 60, or 70, or even 80. Some of my best times were during the 10 years that Gus and Margaret and I were together. I guess it all depends upon what you want and expect out of life.

I'm not sure if I was all that good in bed or not. Margaret always seemed to like what I did. I never saw Gus do too much different than I did.

Actually, he did get Margaret to enjoy it when he licked her down below. She never liked it much before when she was younger, so I had given up trying. Gus finally talked her into letting him do it, and she really, really liked it. He called it, "licking the rose petals clean."

One of the next times we had sex—just Margaret and me—she asked me to lick her rose petals, too. I liked doing it. Before it was over, she had grabbed me by the back of my head and was pushing me harder and harder into her crotch. I could hardly keep my tongue going or get breaths. But when she climaxed, it was amazing to be right down there in the midst of the action! For that kind of reaction and how good it felt for her to get so excited, I could put up with a little hair-pulling.

We did it orally a lot after that, and she started doing it to Gus and me, too. I must say that I really enjoyed doing it and having her do it to me. Yes, Gus had a name for that, too—"eatin' the rattlesnake." He always had a funny way of saying things, even back when we were kids. When Margo asked him why he called it that, he just laughed and said, "Margaret, it's because you just never know when the rattlesnake will strike!"

I've got good ole Gus to thank for those rose petal, hair pulling, rattlesnake and "choo-choo train" memories that are mighty good to think about when I'm diddling myself these days. I even miss the back-scratching.

I'd like to have it again—both with the mouth and inside some nice woman—but if not, I've had it pretty good already. Actually, I've had it double-good, if you count the years with Gus doing it with Margaret, sort of like eating your cake and having it, too. That's more than a lot of men can say.

ARTHUR & MAMIE (BOTH 78)
PEACHES & DREAMS

"The healthier we've become, we've seen it translate into better and better sex. We try to stay very active. We do things all the time to keep the romance alive. I think it's really that simple—you either keep the fire burning or it goes out."
—ARTHUR

(1) What is your age, background and general health?

MAMIE

We're both 78 years old. Arthur comes from a long line of Kentucky farmers and horse breeders. For privacy's sake, I don't want to mention how many, but let me just mention that several of the farm's horses have won the Derby, as well as many other races. He has passed most of his operations on down to his children and grandchildren now. He is still a gentleman farmer with a wonderful historic home and lots of memories from past days. He lost his wife Eulabelle five years ago.

I am from a long line of well-known furniture makers, and I was married to John, also from a long line of well-known furniture manufacturers, for 55 years until he passed away five years ago.

Arthur and I met over four years ago, when both of us were 74, at a health resort.[4*] Even though we came from different parts of

4 * EDITOR'S NOTE: The resort mentioned in this chapter is very prestigious and expensive, maintains rigorous application standards, has an extensive waiting list of clients and does little commercial advertising; therefore, the resort owner has respectfully requested that we avoid mentioning the name of the resort for all the obvious reasons. Since a selected number of interviews for the Seasoned Romance™ Book Series have

the South, nearly 500 miles apart, it's amazing how many things we share. We both lost spouses to unhealthy lifestyles—alcohol, tobacco and too much of the wrong kinds of food. As both of us grieved following the losses of our spouses, each of us were encouraged to get started with exercise and wellness programs to help us through the darkest times. And then, after each of us was a half-year into a better and more fit lifestyle, we decided to spend time at a health resort that caters to seniors who, like us, are wanting to learn more about longevity, wellness, eating better and physical fitness.

There really isn't a lot of time to socialize the first few days you are at this resort, especially in this particular program. You check into your private room, then you go through a lot of tests and examinations, then you are placed in groups of five and work with a trainer who explains everything to you and makes sure you get where you are supposed to be at the right time.

Mostly, you do a lot of walking and controlled fasting the next few days. They have different natural hot springs there, as well as more modern spas and baths. Every day, from the first day, you go through bodywork,

---

been conducted at this resort, we have agreed, of course, to honor that request.

which is deep tissue massage, for at least an hour. Then you go through at least another hour of more gentle Swedish-type massage.

Many of the people there, like me, were in the process of making pretty drastic lifestyle and wellness changes, so there is also an emphasis on hands-on classes in food choices and preparation, fitness and exercise, as well as dealing with emotional issues such as grief and hurt. There are counselors there, too, to deal with deeper issues.

Every morning started with a chapel and Bible class, which I really enjoyed. That's where I first noticed Arthur. It was the second or third day we were there. I remember that he looked dashing in his white jogging suit and nice tan. Even sitting down, he simply had that look of aristocracy. He is completely white-haired with a very Kentucky-ish moustache and Van Dyke beard, so he definitely turns a woman's head.

I counted 30 or so "champions," as the staff called us. We spent time together at meals and individual recreation periods, but I didn't really say much to Arthur the first few days.

During the free time in the afternoon, you are encouraged to spend time alone writing in your journal and thinking through all the new information you are receiving. Some people do this in their dorm room. Some go swimming and do their homework by the pool. Others play tennis and keep a notebook handy to use during breaks.

The weather was warm and absolutely beautiful, so I decided that I wanted to walk on one of the nature trails every day, then sit on one of the many wood benches along the path and do my homework.

That's where I first spent any time with Arthur. He had decided to do the same thing as me, and came walking along as I was writing in my journal. I must admit that my pulse quickened. He seemed to have that effect on me even back then, no matter where I saw him.

There is something so regal about Arthur. He is imperially slender and has the warmest, friendliest brown eyes I've ever seen. His hair, moustache and beard looked even whiter up close. And that first day, the one thing I couldn't take my eyes off was his lips as he talked. He has beautiful white teeth that flash when he smiles or talks, but it was his lips that really caught my eye. I've always loved kissing, even back to my teenage years, so maybe that's why his lips were so attractive to me.

He stopped for a few moments, and we made a little small talk. It was nothing important, just friendly-like. Then he walked on down the path to the next bench to do his journaling. I watched him walk away until he was out of sight. It was such a manly, stately walk. I realized right then that something was happening to me. I felt so warm inside— very alive. I really liked him, even though he didn't seem attracted to me at all.

The next day, we did the same thing, only Arthur asked if he could sit with me for awhile. We talked more about where we were from and our shared dreams of getting more fit and learning more about wellness.

Again, I still didn't know if he liked me much or not. We kept meeting that way, then started meeting for meals, then eventually sat next to each other during classes. I tried to "keep my cool," as my grandkids call it, but I was already madly in love with that man. The attraction was so physical for me, too, which surprised me. Both my first husband and myself were very unhealthy for so many years, so that part of our life had diminished, especially during our fifties and sixties. By the time my husband passed away during our early-seventies, the only sex we had was touching each other once in a while and climaxing that way. It was still some- what satisfying, but I often longed for more, and my husband wasn't able to do anything for a longer period of time. I accepted it, of course, and made the best of it, but I wished we could do more.

That's why, when I was around Arthur, and when I started feeling like a highly-aroused teenager when I was with him, I was probably the most surprised person in the world. I didn't think 74 year old ladies felt like that anymore.

And then I had to keep dealing with the guilt of feeling that way about a man so soon after my husband passed away. I tried to be the grieving widow, even at the wellness resort, but I felt more like a butterfly emerging from a cocoon.

The problem was still that I couldn't tell anyone about these feelings, certainly not Arthur.

ARTHUR

It's almost comical now to hear Mamie talk like this, because I was going through almost identical feelings—the resurgent feelings and even the guilt.

My wife and I had been so unhealthy during the past 20 years or so, and when she got sick during our early seventies, our sex life, or what was left of it that the bad food and unhealthy habits had diminished greatly, had almost completely vanished. Oh, I still had some of the same old feelings, but I didn't act much on them, even playing with myself. I just felt too old, and didn't think you were supposed to feel like that anymore.

That's why, as I got more concerned about wellness, and especially after I went to the health resort and met Mamie, it was like an entirely new set of feelings coming over me. It wasn't exactly the same as when I was 13 or 14, learning about sex and going through all the emotions and discoveries, but it was very similar.

Plus, with losing weight and being slender again, even looking at myself in the mirror was emotionally rewarding. I had barely looked at myself for years. I felt alive again!

When I hear Mamie say now how much she liked me, yet she wasn't sure if I felt the same way, I can only relate what was going on. I was never able to express myself very openly. Men in my family, or any men that I knew, were pretty close-lipped when it came to feelings. Maybe it's particularly a Southern peculiarity, perhaps. My mother was a proper Bostonian who had met and fell in love with my Kentucky-born-and-bred father when he attended Harvard. When she moved to the Bluegrass State after they married, she felt sometimes like she had fallen off the edge of the earth. That made her more determined than ever to rear my brothers and me in the blue-blooded ways of being a gentleman, of not acting lower-class by whooping and hollering. It carried over to the other areas of my life.

It even carried over to our horse-breeding and races. I remember my mother saying, "A gentlemen says little when he wins, and he says even less when he loses." We won some of the biggest races, and we lost quite a few, but we never forgot what we were taught.

I wouldn't change a thing about my childhood, but it definitely made me less expressive than other men, perhaps.

What Mamie didn't know, and what I wasn't able to express to her right then, was that while she thought I was being "cool" and unfeeling, I was actually trying to avoid letting her know what she was doing to me. Every time I was around her, and especially when I got up to leave her, I was glad for the journaling book that I carried around, since I invariably became aroused. I felt like a teenager again, and I must admit that it felt very good to be so alive. I loved the elegant way she carried herself. I could feel my insides start to warm just from remembering her perfume and smile. She was definitely having an effect on me, and I liked how it made me feel.

I remember sometimes back in the room looking at myself in the full-length mirror, especially after I got out of the shower, and seeing what all these new emotions were doing to my manhood. Being slender made my maleness look bigger and longer. I can't imagine a guy not liking that.

I just didn't know how to say anything to Mamie. She was the first woman, other than my wife, for whom I felt such a strong attraction.

(2) Is sex still a part of your life, and, if so, how has it (and you) changed over the years?

ARTHUR

We've been involved intimately from the first week we met. I wouldn't say any of this if you hadn't agreed to change most of the details. We come from families who tend to shy away from personal publicity, and I would never bear to see Mamie's family or my family hurt in any way.

The truth is, we actually went much farther with sex from the beginning than either of us ever expected. It started out pretty innocently, just sitting beside each other.

One day I asked her to go riding on one of the tandem bicycles that were always available at the spa. We took along a small basket of cold cider and a fresh-baked loaf of multigrain bread. We found a remote meadow. I put a blanket down beside a nearby tree and stream. We spent most of the afternoon relaxing, talking and listening to the bubbling brook.

After we ate a snack, I sat back against a tree to do my journal and promptly fell asleep. When I woke up, Mamie was on her side, also asleep, using my thigh as a pillow for her head. It felt so natural to be with her. When she stirred, I started touching her shoulders and neck. She smiled at me, then put her hand on my leg.

I was already aroused, but that did it. I don't think she meant her gesture as overtly sexual, but my private parts didn't know that. When she rolled around, her head still on my thigh, to look up at me, I guess my impulses were increasingly evident. I had a thin jogging suit on, so there wasn't much left to imagination.

Then she did something that really surprised me. She reached up and touched me there, tentatively at first, then more openly until it was evident that both of us had forever crossed some kind of invisible barrier.

For me, it was "off to the races." I just hoped it was a run for the roses, so to speak.

MAMIE

To this day, I still can't believe I was so forward with Arthur that afternoon when we went for the bicycle ride. I just know that it was something that had built up inside me that week. Then on our way to the stream, I was on the back seat of the bicycle, watching Arthur as he pedaled. He told me that it was the first time he had ridden a bike in at least 50 years. I just loved everything about him—the way he moved, the way he was willing to push himself to get into better shape. As we pedaled, I kept getting more and more aroused. I became aware that even the bicycle seat was rubbing me in the right places as we rode through the woods. I didn't know where all these feelings and sensations were coming from or where they were leading. I just knew that I liked the way it made me feel.

Again, I honestly didn't know I could ever experience those feelings and sensations again. I felt more alive out there in the sunshine pedaling with a man I had only met a few days before than I had felt in years.

When he fell asleep, I wrote in my journal for awhile, then I decided to lay against his leg and rest. It felt nice to be so close to him, and I must admit that my dreams that afternoon were mostly about him. When I woke up, he was stroking my shoulders. It took me a few seconds to figure out where I was. When I turned around to look up at his face, the sight I saw right in front of me was ample indication that he was becoming as aroused as I was.

To this day, I still can't believe I was so forward with him, reaching up and touching his hardness. I don't remember ever doing that with John, since he mostly initiated everything when it came to sex.

All I know is that when it happened, something totally wonderful connected between Arthur and myself. I couldn't hold myself back anymore, or maybe I just didn't want to. In some ways, it had been building up since I had known Arthur, but in other ways it was something had been building up for years.

Certainly, we were two consenting adults who could do anything we wanted, but here were a Baptist deacon and a Methodist Sunday School teacher, both of us 74 years old, acting like rambunctious teenagers out on a date. Or, maybe we simply realized that we didn't want to miss out on each other, I don't know. I could hardly breathe at that point, much less think. It happened so quickly and washed over both of us like a tidal wave.

Mainly what I remember from that point were his kisses. We touched each other a lot, kissing most of the time while our hands undressed each other. We both had jogging suits on, so the undressing part wasn't difficult. He was so manly, but in a gentle sort of way. Nothing about him threatened me at all. As he began to caress me, murmuring as he touched my breasts, then moved down to explore my body, I felt such an explosion of emotions and sensations that I didn't know were inside me. He seemed to like the way my body responded to him, and he especially liked it when I stroked and kissed him in all the right places.

When he finally went inside me, it was the most complete feeling in the world. And my leaner body was nice, too. I had more energy than I'd had in years. It was surprising how good it all went. And he was masterful, such a gentleman.

A few moments ago he said he hoped it was a run for the roses, which is something I guess you would expect from a man who lived his life around thoroughbreds. I can tell you that he showed, placed and won—all in one race. I couldn't believe how good he was and how wonderful it felt.

When it was over, and he was still lying lightly on top of me, it seemed so natural for him to be there with me, inside me. When he finally slid out and rolled over beside me, I already knew that I couldn't wait for the next time. I hoped he felt the same way about me, for I was hopelessly, helplessly and passionately in love with this man.

We ended up spending two weeks together at the resort. During the remainder of the time, we made love several more times. One time we even lay on an isolated, grassy meadow, completely nude, and did it to each other with our tongues and mouths. I couldn't believe I was so forward. I had heard of that sort of thing, but I had never done anything oral like that in my entire life.

Maybe some of these memories wouldn't be as important to some people, but to two 74-year-olds, it was spectacular. We were feeling healthier than ever, partly from the program we were going through, but mostly because we had found each other. It was as if all the negative things in our lives were being released and discarded, while these wonderful and positive things were rushing in.

We got married three months later. During the interim, I visited his home several times, he visited mine, plus we took a vacation together to Key West. I'm not saying what we did was right, and I wouldn't recommend it for everyone. In fact, I was pretty much a prude most of my life.

I still believe the worst thing kids can do is run out, get involved sexually and rush into marriage. I guess that makes it so ironic that Arthur and I did exactly the opposite of what either of us said we believed. But it was like we had found soul mates, not just sexual partners. It kept getting better and better.

I realize that all the things I'm saying could be used by any hot-blooded 18-year-old wanting to justify hopping into bed with another hot-blooded 18-year-old. All I know is that it was driven by a love that was so strong and powerful, like the waves of the sea.

I must admit, though, that we both felt guilty for being together intimately without being married. That's one reason we went ahead with the wedding so soon.

(3) If you are currently involved in an intimate relationship, how long has it lasted? What has made it last? What have been the best (or worse) parts of the relationship?

MAMIE

We've been married now for four years. We are still very involved intimately. If anything, I'm enjoying it more than I ever remember at any time in my life. I don't want to throw stones at my first husband John, for he was a wonderful man in so many ways, but the only way I can explain how great love is with Arthur is to share a little of the past with my first husband. John was an in-and-out type of guy. He got charged up in a hurry, went inside quickly, was pretty quiet, even during the most passionate moments. More often than not, he went off inside me, hugged me a moment or so, then fell asleep quickly and left me to finish myself off with a finger or—later in life—a small, quiet, egg-shaped vibrator I kept discreetly in my bedside table.

John and I talked about a lot of things—especially about our children and the furniture business, but he never wanted to discuss much about intimacy, so we let so many things go unspoken. He wasn't interested in exploring new positions, other than him on top. He didn't really want to do much foreplay, other than a few kisses and a few touches on my breasts. He wanted to go right inside. I hardly ever experienced any kind of deep feelings or orgasm with him. I liked the feeling of being connected with him and the warm wetness deep inside afterward, but that was about it.

I guess that's pretty blunt to say, and I don't want to make John out to be anything other than a wonderful husband, provider and father. He was a very smart, handsome, hard-working man who was always considered a "catch." He just was never too concerned about satisfying me. I was brought up to be a true blue Southern belle who believed that satisfying my husband brought great satisfaction to myself in all the other areas of life, so in many ways I couldn't have been happier.

He was a pretty big guy, heavier especially toward the end of his life, so sex eventually became more of a chore to him than a real pleasant experience. In his defense, for a lot of the years we were married, I didn't know enough nor was I able to tell him how to please me. I just figured that it was my fault, or that was all there was to it, and in the end finishing myself off after he fell asleep wasn't such a bad thing for me. He was such a sound sleeper.

Doing myself always felt good, and often, after I climaxed by myself as he lay sleeping, I would roll over and lie next to John. In some ways, I wished he would pay more attention to my needs, but in other ways, I was so happy to be married to such a wonderful man, and I felt a little guilty for wanting more from him or more from life.

There were so many great things about our marriage that the one part that seems lacking was very small in comparison. There was a lot of prestige being part of a well-established furniture family—both before and after marriage. We had a very nice life, went to the big international furniture market in North Carolina, where two times a year we spent several weeks there in a flurry of parties and meetings, generally enjoying time with old friends and receiving gracious reviews of our new lines of furniture. All that translated into even greater sales for the next year, which was even more of a reason to prepare for the next market and all the great times there.

In-between, we reared our children, enjoying all the school, social and athletic activities that go along with being community leaders and respected business owners. I can say thankfully that our kids never gave a moment of worry as they went through school, then college, then becoming a part of our furniture business.

So when I say there were times that I wanted more out of life, it wasn't anything to do with our lifestyle. John literally devoted his life to providing the best for me and our children. He was the best when it came to that.

That's why I always felt almost ungrateful when I thought about our sex life. It's not as if I ever felt a temptation to cheat on him. I would have never done that.

Still, there were those moments when I finished myself off and lay beside John, listening to him breathe so deeply, that I sometimes wondered if that was all it would ever be and if I was the reason that it wasn't any better.

And I say all that, not to disparage John at all, but just to let you know how I felt then and how it compares today.

With Arthur, intimacy has been quite different. He is a very thorough person. He pays a lot of attention to details in every area of his life. He's wonderful that way in bed. He spends however much time it takes to make me satisfied, and it is delightful to feel that he is enjoying all the foreplay as much as I am.

And for a man who is pretty quiet, he's such a romantic. I like that, because I've always been a romantic person. I've said before that I'm a true-blue Southern belle at heart, and I think there's a bit of Scarlett O'Hara in most women born in Dixie. Okay, I don't look a bit like Maureen Sullivan, but if Clark Gable was still living, was 78 years old, had white hair, a white moustache and Van Dyke beard, that would be Arthur, for sure. So I really feel quite a bit like I'm living on Tara, even if it's surrounded by Kentucky bluegrass.

ARTHUR

Now she's got me embarrassed. I'm afraid that from the things you've heard Mamie say, she's painted me as the handsome one and her as the ugly duckling. Nothing could be farther from the truth. She's actually the one with such elegance and beauty. She has eyes that light up an entire room. Her face is so perfectly formed. I just love everything about her, and it has been that way pretty much from the first time I spied her at the health resort.

I didn't know anything about her, but there was a connection from the beginning.

I didn't know her when she was younger, of course, but she has told me that she never got totally satisfied during her first marriage, and that part of it was that she didn't express herself very well to let John know what she wanted.

I was in just the opposite situation. My wife Eulabelle was, as her name implies, a true Southern belle in every way. In public, she was a perfect lady. But in private she was more of a "steel magnolia." She was very expressive and determined about what she wanted. In our younger days, she wanted sex as much as I did, which was fine by me. We had a good sex life, but as we both got older and more unhealthy, it sort of fell by the wayside. We reached the point that nothing I did seemed to please her.

When I would try to initiate anything, Eulabelle would say, "Oh, for goodness sake, Art. We're both too old for that sort of thing!"

After awhile, I thought, "Why bother?" She wasn't happy or satisfied, no matter what I did, and I ended up frustrated at her and myself. I didn't blame her, even then, since towards the end, a lot of the bad effects were from the medicines she was taking and her illnesses.

I never did cheat on her. I really did take the "for better or worse" part seriously when I said our vows, and as we got older, I just assumed that life balances things out, and this was definitely some of the "worse." I loved Eulabelle and was willing to go through whatever happened as her health got worse. In some ways, a part of me died during those last years together. I never thought it would come back again.

Being with Mamie has been very different for me, especially with both of us moving toward very healthy lifestyles. Both of us are getting to learn all over again how to satisfy and be satisfied. I think that's what has made our relationship so special. And I am in awe at how wonderful it is now.

(4) What details about you, your partner and your sexual relationship would surprise people if they knew?

ARTHUR

I was always taught that a true gentleman never talks about intimate things, but the main reason I would do this would be to encourage other seniors to realize that life isn't over when you lose your spouse or when you reach retirement age. Nor is it over because you have been unhealthy for a long time. I don't believe it's ever too late to turn over a new leaf. I'm living proof that you can make a big change, even later in life.

Specifically, I think the most surprising thing, certainly it has been surprising to me, is how good Mamie and I are in bed. If you could have only known me five or 10 years ago, you wouldn't even recognize me now. From what she says, it's the same for Mamie. Both of us are stronger, younger-acting and more excited about life than ever before.

I can't begin to describe how it makes me feel to know that what I do satisfies her. Every time we do it is different, of course, but overall she seems like everything I do is perfect and pleasing. That makes me feel like a million bucks. What guy wouldn't feel like a Kentucky thoroughbred stud with his filly thoroughly enjoying every romp in the hay?

And the healthier we've become—the resort where we met was just one of many good things we've done for ourselves—we've seen it translate into better and better sex. We try to stay very active. We do things all the time to keep the romance alive. I think it's really that simple—you either keep the fire burning or it goes out. Thankfully, even if it appears to have gone out, it IS possible to rekindle the fire and have it flame brighter than ever before. That's certainly the case with me.

I've done a lot of reading about this in the past couple of years, and I've seen that the major difference between a young and an older person, in terms of sex, is not the plumbing but the brain. Seniors often get in ruts and stop thinking about sex. Then they stop being excited about sex.

Not Mamie and me. Not now, at least. We've talked about this a lot, and we've decided to do whatever we can to satisfy each other as long as we can, even if it forces us out of the comfort zones we often get accustomed to. That would definitely surprise people who knew us before we met each other.

As Mamie mentioned, we light candles beside the bed. We give long, erotic massages. We take showers and baths together. We touch each other all the time throughout the day and especially at night. We have romantic dinners with Nat King Cole, the Glenn Miller Band, Johnny Mathis, Patti Page or some other beautiful music playing in the background.

Sometimes we even video our lovemaking so we can enjoy it later. How shocking is that?

MAMIE

A surprising story? Here's one that I remember with especial fondness: We went to Key West for our honeymoon. Naturally, it was hot and humid, even in the nice resort where we stayed. One night after we spent the afternoon in the pool and beach, I rang room service and ordered a nice meal for us. Arthur was taking a late afternoon nap, and was still sleeping when the food arrived. The server got the table prepared, then left.

Arthur was still napping, so I decided to surprise him. He talks a lot about how he enjoys looking at my body and touching it.

We were both getting pretty fit by then. I took my clothes off, then went over and shook him gently. As he woke up, I sat down at the table, crossed my legs, and as seductively as possible, in my best Mae West voice, asked him, "What's your pleasure, mister?"

We both laughed, but I could tell that he enjoyed the view. He came over and kissed me, then touched my breasts. Impulsively, I told him to take off his clothes and join me at the table. I was surprised when he did. I wasn't sure someone as proper as he was would do something like that. Frankly, I couldn't believe what I was doing.

We ate together, with the candles flickering. It was very sensual to me, and I could tell that he was getting warm, too.

Neither of us have desserts much anymore except on special occasions, but that night the meal came with the most beautiful spice cake covered with the most luscious-smelling peach brandy sauce.

Arthur kept looking at me slyly, so I did something even more impulsive than merely eating in the nude, even as erotic as that seemed. I ran a fingertip through the peach sauce and touched it to my tongue. Not to be outdone, he grinned and did the same thing.

Well, I couldn't stop at that without topping what he'd done, so I put my fingertip back in the sauce and drizzled it around my nipples. He followed suit, then raised the ante by smearing it into his pure white chest hair.

I didn't know what to do next, so I stood up and put some of the sauce around my navel. He stood up and put some of the sauce all over his maleness, and he grinned in a challenging way that seemed to dare me to do something even better.

I couldn't believe our little peachy game had gone this far, but I couldn't back off, so I went over and licked the sauce off his nipples. He did the same to me, then he knelt over and licked my navel area, smacking his lips as if it were the best dessert in the world.

By that time, we moved over to the bed. He went to the bathroom and wet a washcloth to wash himself off. I'm still amazed at how forward I was with him on this, but I told him to stop and gestured for him to lie on the bed. I wasn't sure what it would be like, but I went ahead and licked off all the peach sauce on his chest hair, then down below. The peach brandy sauce tasted great, of course, and I could tell that he was really enjoying it because I kept making noises, too. I could see very literally that he was enjoying it when I licked up and down his gorgeous shaft.

Afterward, we made love with him on top, but several times that night he told me how much he liked being touched with my tongue. As with John and myself, Arthur and his wife Eulabelle had never done anything oral, either.

That night, while I watched him sleeping, I decided to do him all the way orally the next time we did it, just as I had done in the meadow at the health resort. I had enjoyed watching him getting so aroused during the time before.

The next day we spent all day in a fishing boat with a number of other people, and we were both extremely tired by the time we got back to our room.

But the day after that was more relaxed. I kept looking at him as he read the newspaper on the covered cabana outside our room. He had a pair of loose swimming trunks on, and the way he sat with his legs crossed at the knee, I could see the white mesh sack inside his trunks that held his privates. For some reason, it seemed so sensual to me, even though I couldn't see much of the real thing, but the delicious thoughts started to make my pulse quicken. He couldn't see me looking at him, since he was reading the paper so intently. I kept trying to read my historical romance novel, yet, which made me even more aroused.

Maybe it was the honeymoon. Maybe it was Key West. Maybe it was the way it felt to have Arthur on top of me, kissing me with his moustache and Van Dyke. Everything about Arthur made me so excited.

Finally, I walked over to the door to our room, went inside, took off my swimsuit, reached around the door and tossed my swimsuit onto his legs. He was a bit shocked and had that little boy dazed look that a man gets when you interrupt him reading his newspaper.

I asked him, Mae West-like, "Hey, big boy, why don't you come in heah and give this gal a good time?" He put his paper down. I knew I had his attention. I went inside and waited for him. He came in and asked what I wanted. I had him sit on a big love seat, knelt down and began doing him orally while at the same time I was stroking his shaft with my hand as fast as I could. Suddenly he began breathing real hard and then climaxed in my mouth.

I love it! I like the taste of his liquid, the sexy way he pulsates inside my mouth and how I can give him such grand pleasure. I find the whole process to be a real turn-on for me.

And I especially like it because he has grown to really enjoy returning the favor.

When we do it orally now, sometimes he goes first, then me. And sometimes it's the other way around. Either way is tantalizing.

I don't know if I like it because neither of us ever did it that way before we met, or if it is because it's so...I don't even know the words to describe it. Maybe exotic and sensual. I just know I like it, and I can tell that he does, too!

I'm sure this sort of thing would really surprise people if they knew either of us. On the other hand, I'm not sure how surprised people would be anymore. Both Arthur and I have gone from being out-of-shape old fogies to in-shape 70-ish people who love life, romance and each other. We've gone from being lonely to being happily married. Still, I don't think anyone who knew us before would think in a million years that it could be so good in bed, certainly not me, nor Arthur.

All I know is that I don't know how many years we'll have together, and I want to make all the time we have very special. And I'd like to have a lot more peach brandy sauce times, too, if you know what I mean!

(5) In your opinion, what is the secret to being a seasoned, sensual senior and what is one story you would like to tell that would help people understand how special sex can be to people over 60?

MAMIE

You want another story to top that one? I'll have to think about that. Better yet, Arthur can probably come up with one that's about how special sex can be.

Mainly I'd say that I definitely think that sex can be special to people our age. And I hope it gets even better for Arthur and me. We have some friends whom we got to know at the wellness resort where we met. They are both in their mid-eighties, yet they are so sweet on each other. They are always holding hands. He calls her "Miss America." She calls him "Mr. Universe" and pats his bicep. They call each other "My Lover." They are just so passionate. It you only met them once, you might think they were putting on an act, but we've been around them quite a bit, and they are that passionate toward each other all the time. They are so devoted to making each day special and spicing things up for the other. Even during the week at the resort, they were always going to one of their rooms to spend the afternoon together, then they would come back to lunch more lovey-dovey than ever. We spent part of the weekend with them during the last Kentucky Derby, and they are still like frisky teenagers.

So I think sex can be special as seniors, but only if you discover the *real* fountain of youth, which is exercise, eating right, romance and having the right attitude about life.

And our eightysomething friends are living proof that being romantic is a choice that you make every day.

ARTHUR

What Mamie says about the fountain of youth is surely true. Exercise is important. Eating right is essential. We're both loving the effects of herbs, vitamins and minerals. I think they are vital to a good life and great sex. I've used a couple of herbal "male enhancement" products, and they often make the feelings even more intense, which is always great. But we've learned that spending time in a health food store and the exercise room is more important to our intimate life than anything.

As for sex, I think being more seasoned is definitely an advantage, as long as you don't get stuck in your ways. I'm saying that as a man who was in a rut for far too many years. I'm glad I woke up and started smelling the roses before it was too late.

It means spending time thinking about what pleases your mate. Mamie is so good at this. I'm trying to get better. But it's not just about the sexual act. It's just about being thoughtful and respectful toward each other.

Even back in my youth, I cringed when I'd hear some guy call his girlfriend or wife "My Old Lady," "The Ball and Chain" or other phrases like that. How could a woman truly respect that? For that matter, what does it say about the guy?

Okay, I've preached enough. I just want to say that being at this place in my life with Mamie is special, too. She has made everything so wonderful. I thank God every day for bringing the two of us together.

She's always full of surprises. You asked for an example of how special our sex life is today, so let me tell you one that just happened recently. We travel quite a bit anymore, and not long ago we were at a cozy bed and breakfast place out in Montana. The area was breathtaking, and the air was incredibly fresh. We had been planning the week for some time, but I didn't know that Mamie had planned a little more than I knew about.

She always likes to wear sexy negligees at night, whether we have plans to actually be intimate or not. So on the first night in Montana, she didn't surprise me too much when she appeared wearing a peach-colored little thing with furry pieces and all. I liked it a lot, but I didn't yet know that there was more. She also had bought some peach champagne. She asked if I remembered the peach brandy sauce down in Key West.

Did I? That was one of my all-time best sexual memories with her.

That night she put a large towel down on the bed, then had me lay down on my stomach. She dabbed the champagne all over my back and began licking it with her tongue. As if that wasn't enough, then she did the same thing to my front. She didn't do just my body, but my moustache and beard, too. That was very sensual as she licked the champagne around my face.

If you would have asked me a few years ago, I would have never imagined liking something like what I'm describing.

Today, I can tell you that I do like it. I truly do. And she couldn't have picked a better scent than peaches. Not only did it remind me of the time in Key West, but peaches have always been my favorite fruit since I was a little child. It's been the same all the years since then. I love that smell.

By the time she got to my legs, then started moving in for the best part, I could hardly stand it. The feelings were so intense. I thought I would purely explode. She began doing incredible things with her mouth, and the peach smell lingering all around us only made it more exciting.

After she finished me off so delightfully, I did the same thing to her with the peach champagne, back and front, then finished her off with a finger that I dipped in the bubbly, then my tongue. It was kind of kinky, I suppose, especially for 78 year old kids, but it sure was nice, too.

We did take a shower before we went to bed that night, since we didn't want to wake up smelling like day-old peach champagne. No matter, since the incredible peach aroma filled the room, only adding to the memorable evening.

I wish I could describe with more eloquence how special that night was to both of us, mainly because it reminded us of how far we have come together—to be able to share something so fun, so erotic and so intimate.

I remember after the shower as we snuggled together on the bed, still smelling the fragrant peach champagne. I listened to her breathe as she fell asleep, and I lay there for a long time with my heart so overflowing with love for this woman. I thanked God again and again for the wonderful gift named Mamie He had given to me.

Both of us used to be unhealthy and stuck in our own ruts. Thanks to our relationship with each other, we have come such a long way.

And I believe it's going to keep getting better. We're living the kind of life together that dreams are made of...or maybe I should say peaches and dreams!

CHUCK (70) & THELMA (67)
Minister's Suit

"I've never cheated on her, though there are plenty of times I could—as any minister or public figure can tell you. I don't intend to cheat on her. That's something I simply don't want to do, because I grew up in a family where my father did

it a lot. He was a traveling salesman, and the stories about him were legendary."
—**CHUCK**

(1) What is your age, background and general health?

CHUCK

I am 70, and Thelma is 67. For awhile, right after I finished Bible school, I traveled with a fairly well-known Southern Gospel quartet. Then, once we started making babies, we both realized that I needed to settle down. I have been a pastor in churches since then. We took our first pastorate in a tiny little church, and worked our way up to one of the largest in our denomination. Five years ago, I retired from my last pastorate and now just travel to speaking engagements 30 or so weekends a year.

As for health, we are pretty fit. I played football and basketball in high school and did a lot of intramural sports in college, so I've always enjoyed working out. Thelma has some medical problems now, but she takes medicine and is able to live a very normal life.

I jog several miles a day, no matter where I am that day. I still like Thelma's meals too much, and I found out a long time ago that jogging was the only way I could keep the waist slim and my body working well, yet still enjoy her good food.

(2) Is sex still a part of your life, and, if so, how has it (and you) changed over the years?

CHUCK

We enjoy sex, but not as much as I would like. Let me quickly explain that a long time ago, Thelma and I really got open enough to talk about the fact that we simply had different appetites. Thelma enjoys it more when we only do it a time or two each week; she says that it is more intense for her then. I could be happy if I had sex at least once a day or more, even now.

I guess you could use the analogy that she prefers quality, while I like quantity. That's over-simplifying it, of course.

When we were first married, I needed it several times a day. Needless to say, she thought that was pretty extreme.

From research I've done, especially for our age, I realize that my appetite is still somewhat high, but I've grown to understand that I was made the way I am, and it's up to me to find positive ways to deal with the situation.

To my way of thinking, the problem isn't the sex drive. It's what you do with it. Frankly, it's a good problem to have, if you ask me. The times when Thelma is ready for sex are so good that they make up for the other times when I want it and don't get it by going inside her. She's a very good lover when she's ready, but it's simply not as important to her as it is to me. And it has always been very important to me.

Once we got honest about how different we were, we also agreed that cheating wasn't an option—not just because of my position in the church, but also because it's something that would have torn us apart. I'd already seen it happen too many times to college friends, guys in the traveling music groups, people in churches and even some of my colleagues.

So I'm extremely happy and even proud to tell you without reservation that I've never cheated on Thelma through all these years. Yes, there were plenty of times I could have— as any public figure can tell you.

Cheating on her was something I simply refused to do to her, mainly because I grew up in a family with a father who did it a lot.

He was a traveling salesman, as people used to call them back in those days, and the stories about him were legendary. I heard more about it as I got older because we had the same name—Senior and Junior. He was a "cat-daddy," as they used to say. He was some piece of work, that man.

I don't know if his success in so many beds was because of the size of his tool, the way he used it, his charm or what. Anytime I saw him as a kid—walking in as he was getting dressed or when he took a leak when we were hunting or fishing—he naturally looked huge to me, but whether he was endowed better than others, I couldn't really tell you. All I knew as I grew older is that he obviously had a talent for delighting members of the female gender and used it often.

Apparently I got my appetite naturally. It's just that we used that gift differently.

I'm pretty sure my mother knew what was going on, but she didn't leave him—for whatever reason. I couldn't believe that she stuck with him through thick and thin, especially if she did know, but I learned to accept it and tried to get on with my life without ill will towards either parent.

My brother and I knew about him and his hefty appetite for young women, especially once we were teenagers. It was impossible not to know. I helped out in his office two summers before I headed to college, and there were women who would call and leave messages that left little to the imagination.

One of the first times it happened I confronted him about it. He just smiled, winked mischievously and said, "Chuckie, ole boy, that's the way real men do things. Your Mama understands how it is with a man who has needs. Her dad was like that. My dad was like that. You'll probably be a chip off the old block, too. You'll understand it better as you get older."

He also told me, "Don't mention any of this to Mom, since bringing up the subject will only embarrass her if she knows that you know. Man up, old boy, and keep your mouth shut."

That was that. End of discussion.

One other time when we talked about it, he said he loved Mom dearly and planned to stay married to her forever, but then he grinned and told me that it was hard to stick with "the main dish" when life was such "a beautiful buffet of bodacious women out there." He actually used those words. I could have decked him, but figured it wouldn't do any good. He was obviously going to do whatever he wanted.

Quite simply, Dad was the kind of man who could charm the bark off trees—tall, dark and handsome—always with a big wad of money in his pocket and a dazzling white smile on his tanned face. To me, and apparently to others, he was bigger than life. People often tell me how much they like my voice as I preach, but I have no problem admitting that Dad's voice was much better than mine will ever be—deeper and more resonant. When he spoke to civic organizations or company get-togethers, as he sometimes did, he was amazingly captivating. He was quick-witted, always had a great joke ready, was a sharp dresser and great dancer. He could stroke a mean guitar, play violin like a virtuoso, and sang anything from "My Old Kentucky Home" to "The Twelfth of Never" with a voice that sounded like a smoky blend of Mel Tormé, Nat King Cole and Gentleman Jim Reeves. He even traveled for awhile as a young musician and singer playing honky-tonks and barnyard dances, but he eventually decided that he liked sales more than the grind of grimy one-nighters in search of that "neon rainbow" that Alan Jackson sang about much later.

It was probably a good financial decision. He did real well financially all his life, so he always had the latest model Cadillac and custom-tailored suits, even as he got older.

And he certainly had more than his share of groupies enjoyed by the band mates in the group that stuck together after he left, some of whom eventually did pretty well in the music business.

He definitely enjoyed the ladies, and he didn't mend his ways until he was well into his seventies. Even up until that time, I heard stories about him that would curl your hair—including a preference for very young women, the younger the better, and sometimes several of them at a time, even as he got older, much older. I'm not talking jail-bait young, but awfully close to it.

His sales work often brought him in contact with the colleges and universities throughout the four states in his territory. Something about him seemed to attract lots of pretty young coeds, and he used that charm to the hilt. Literally!

I guess the magnetism was exactly what people call it—sex appeal. Anyway, women of all ages dearly loved him and couldn't get enough of him. I guess that's also why my mother didn't leave him. When he was with her, he made her feel like a queen. He always lavished her with the best of everything, from clothing and jewelry to exotic vacations. She absolutely loved to hear him sing and play musical instruments. You could see it in her eyes as she listened so intently to him.

But the one gift he didn't or couldn't give was fidelity. As I said before, if my mother knew about his outside interests, she never let on. If she knew, as he intimated, she obviously made her peace with the situation, no matter the risk or cost.

As I got into my forties and got a little gray in the temples, people used to see my father and myself together and often thought we were brothers. That might seem good to some people, but most of my life it was a real problem, especially with me in the ministry.

Even when I was in my forties and early fifties and sometimes stayed in one of the states where my dad still traveled as a salesman, there were times that I would check into a motel and have some pretty little female desk clerk look at me and my name, then touch my arm and whisper, "Chuck, what's your pleasure tonight?"

I thought I fixed everything when I started signing "Reverend" in front of my name when I checked into hotels and motels. Even then, I had women at different times and places wink slyly and say, "Well, Reverend Chuck, what's your pleasure tonight?" They thought I was putting them on, and that my dad was using "reverend" as some kind of joke. My dad must have been amazing in bed, that's about all I can figure. I'm not even sure I want to know or understand what the attraction was, but apparently it was real and what a lot of women out there wanted a lot of.

I suppose I should be proud of the legacy and DNA that flows through my body, but it sure was a problem for me back then.

For obvious reasons, since I was in the ministry, my Dad never talked about it much to me, even after he became a born-again Christian and straightened his life out during his seventies. The last few years of his life, he and my mother seemed to have very special times. She is still living, so she has told me before that their last years together were the most wonderful of all. I didn't ask a lot of questions, since I don't know how much she knows about all the things he did in his younger days, and I respect her too much to bring all those old things up. That's why I'm only willing to be in this research study if my name and enough details are changed.

I guess it just took my dad a lot of years to realize how destructive his voracious appetite was. Actually, the appetite wasn't destructive, just the way he used his "talents and skills."

After growing up with a real-life Casanova for a father, I simply never wanted to do to my family what he did. He was a good father, in many ways. He was certainly a good provider. He taught us, in his words, to "Work damn hard, then play really damn hard." We had a lot of fun growing up, going on great vacations and playing golf—always one of his great passions—in some of the country's best resorts. Our house was always a magnet for our friends, and they loved it when he played and sang.

I mention all this because I don't want it to seem that he was a totally horrible person. He was very good-hearted and generous, but just seemed to have a mountain-sized sex drive and was an inveterate womanizer.

I also say it because it's part of the explanation of how I have been through the years. I must have gotten more than just my appearance from Dad. I've always had a high level of sexual desire, too. I was a virgin when Thelma and I got married, but only because I had taken the matter into my own hands through my teens and early twenties, so to speak. I always felt a little guilty about pleasuring myself, especially since it was one of those things religious folk never seemed to want to talk about, but I figured it was better than being promiscuous as a single or cheating on a spouse. I still do.

When Thelma and I got married, I thought my problems would be over. In my mind, we would make love like rabbits, I would be thoroughly satisfied, she would think of me as a love god and we would live happily ever after.

Not so. From the beginning, she was shocked that I wanted it so much. I must have seemed like a horrible pervert to her, especially since she was a virgin when we were married, too.

Thankfully, we were able to talk about it openly before it became a wedge between us. I knew that I had to deal realistically and honestly with it—not like my dad did.

The only thing left was sex when she was ready and self-pleasuring when she wasn't. All in all, it worked out well. Best of all, we enjoyed ourselves when we did it together, and I didn't feel guilty about it when we didn't.

It has worked for me, and for us. It keeps me off her back on the days when she isn't interested, but it gives me a release. And as more and more research continues to come out on the subject, it really does seem to be healthy to have an active sex life. God gave sex as a wonderful gift, that's for sure. It's just that we often misuse this gift by thinking that we have to be with other people besides a spouse to enjoy it.

Actually, Thelma has always been pretty creative in this area. At first, when I would play with myself, I would do it in private. Then I finally asked her if she would be embarrassed or uncomfortable if I did it on the bed beside her. She made it very clear that she wouldn't, and soon she seemed to enjoy getting involved in what once was a solo effort.

Since then, she has become a master-ful pleasure giver, touching me all over. Sometimes she even does the stroking on my shaft, which feels great. Although she hasn't always been a great fan of oral sex, through the years she has learned to wield a pretty mean tongue. Even today, when she takes me all the way with her mouth, I go berserk!

Wow! Even as I say this, I realize that has to seem pretty strange for a conservative min-ister. All I know is that it works for us.

As a minister, I can tell you without res-ervation that the Bible has a lot to say about sex and the marriage bed, and God obviously created intimacy as one of the best things in the world when it is cherished as a gift. I always have, and I definitely do today.

(3) If you are currently involved in an inti-mate relationship, how long has it last-ed? What has made it last? What have been the best (or worse) parts of the relationship?

THELMA

We have been together for nearly 50 years. That seems hard to believe, especially since being 70 doesn't seem all that old anymore.

People often say that Chuck and I look 40 or 50. That might be stretching it, but I do think we do look young for him being 70 and me being 67.

The thing that has made life together good for us has been our strong faith and abiding love. Believe it or not, the ministry can be one of the hardest areas to keep a marriage and family together. Not only are you surrounded by people who want you to solve all their problems, but the pastor, especially, is constantly being held up on a pedestal. There's no way to be that perfect.

Then there is lots of pressure to be flawless as his wife, just as there was always pressure on our children to be perfect preacher's kids. We tried to deal with it realistically, knowing that every normal family has flaws and imperfections, but that unrealistic ideal was always an unseen visitor wherever we went. I've seen it destroy some couples and families in a lot of fields—politics, education, business and certainly in the ministry.

Plus, there are women who have been pretty open about their desire to be close, even intimate, with Chuck. Maybe that seems shocking, but there are always people—in any career where leaders are given great honor and respect—who want to be part of it. The ministry is no exception. In fact, because of the spiritual aspect of it, perhaps there are those who truly think that it is their destiny to take their rightful place as his wife. I know this because he has shown me the notes he's received and I've heard him counsel younger ministers on the hazards they face.

Thankfully, he has always handled these things well, and to his credit, he has always sought to include me in all areas of his ministry. That one fact alone has helped keep things very open and healthy.

Also, he has always been very open about staying faithful to me, teaching on the subject of marriage and the absolute necessity of truth from the pulpit, and I have never had one ounce of doubt that he has been true to me. I couldn't handle it if the trust wasn't there.

I think one of the things that has helped us to stay together is his realization, because of his father's past and his own sex drive, that he needed to be very open about his appetites and the women who came on to him.

As Chuck has mentioned, another way that makes it work for us is the fact that we have learned how to appreciate each other and our different sex drives. Now, it's not as if I am a frigid woman who never wants it. Far from it. I can get awfully excited and have lots of fun in bed with Chuck. It's just that doing it all the time seems to make it less exciting when we have intercourse all the time. I get a lot more enjoyment out of it when I let the feelings build up over several days or a week. That's certainly different from Chuck, who always seems ready for action.

I honestly think he enjoys one ejaculation almost as good as the next. In fact, whenever he does two in the same day, he often grins at me and says, "Ah, the second time is always better than the first!" Back in our younger days, he used to say the same thing about the third or fourth times. It became sort of a joke between us.

Once in our early thirties, we were on vacation and our children were with my parents. All alone and able to enjoy just being together with no pressures or outside interruptions, he was almost insatiable. On the very first day, counting the times we did it together and just him, most of the times with my help, I actually saw him climax 18 times. And yes, when I mentioned that it was his eighteenth time, he grinned and said, "Ah, the eighteenth is always better than the first."

He didn't do it but once the second day, if for no other reason than he was a little sore from so much activity the day before. But he quickly regained his appetite, and by the third day he thoroughly enjoyed a dozen times, including two with me. I know this was probably no world record or anything, thought I doubt anyone keeps official track of that sort of thing, but I was amazed to see it with my own eyes, and I am still enthralled at his quick recovery time and how each orgasm seems equally exhilarating to him. It was always so different for me.

I'm certainly not saying all this to make him look bad in any way, nor am I saying it for any other reason than to explain that Chuck was simply given a voracious desire and ability for lots of sex. That's a good thing, but it was quite a challenge as we learned how different we were and how to make it work for both of us without either one feeling guilty or manipulated.

In time, I really grew to enjoy stroking and playing with him, whether we are planning for him to go inside me or not. He is very sensual to me, and when I help give him pleasure, either inside me or with my hand or mouth, it is very satisfying. In fact, a couple of times I got so involved that I actually experienced a climax when he came off in my mouth. I would have never dreamed that sort of thing was even possible if it hadn't happened to me.

It's just that I don't desire it myself as much as he does, not by a long shot, and I enjoy it so much better after the feelings have built up inside me for several days or a week.

(4) What details about you, your partner and your relationship would surprise people if they knew?

CHUCK

Despite our differences in appetites that we've already discussed, I think people would be surprised at how good Thelma and I are in bed together, especially after all these years.

Our society is so conditioned to think of older people and sex as something of a joke. Every comedian, it seems, has a favorite set of jokes about the old guy who can't get it up anymore or the older woman who has no inter-est in romance. I simply choose not to believe those things. Thelma and I have got too many beautiful experiences to allow ourselves to be taken in by all that misinformation.

As for us, I've taught a lot about sex and marriage and romance from the pulpit, and I've counseled lots of my church members on the subject over the years, but people would probably be surprised to know that we enjoy a lot of happiness and romance.

Granted, church folk still tend to see a pastor and his wife as people who walk around with halos and wings or something, never actually experiencing anything real ourselves—good or bad. I can tell you that we have gone through really challenging times, but we also truly do enjoy ourselves together.

Another challenge, if you want to call it a challenge, is that sex isn't something that a pastor can brag about or talk about openly, nor would it be good taste. I wish I could say something about it sometime, though, not so much about myself, of course, but I wish I could tell people how good Thelma is, and about some of the truly glorious times when we have sex.

Maybe I'll write a book about how good sex should be for believers—young and old—someday, especially when you seek to live righteously and as you ask for God's blessings and favor. Truthfully, though, I'm not sure the good folk in the church are ready to read about some of these things in relation to their pastor and wife.

Anyway, what I'm saying is that I wish people could understand how amazing Thelma is. Sometime she catches me completely off guard. There are times, even now, after preaching a sermon as we travel from church to church, that she lets me know in no uncertain terms that she wants to have sex. I probably shouldn't say this, but our secret signal through the years is when she holds my hand and rubs her middle finger very softly in the middle of my palm. When she gives that signal, I know it's time to think about getting back to the motel, if we're traveling, or our home as soon as possible.

On those occasions when we go out to dinner with the host pastor after church, even after she has given me our secret signal, she has actually spent part of the meal rubbing her hand up the inside of my thigh. She sits there looking pious and upright, and meanwhile she's driving me out of my mind. Try talking about wonderful, spiritual things when you are just trying to keep your voice from jumping octaves at all the delicious things she's doing with her fingers!

There have been times, even this past week, during our drive back to our home when she has started taking my clothes off even before I got inside the door. Don't misunderstand me—I'm not complaining at all. I love it, and I don't suppose I'll ever get tired of it.

I guess what I'm trying to say is that she doesn't want sex as much as I do, but whether she does or not, she has a way of making me feel like a super hero. Everywhere I touch her and kiss her, she moans and talks about how good I am. When she pleasures me, she seems to be totally overwhelmed with my pleasure. How can you go wrong with that?

She's such a gift to me, and I've always tried to never take her for granted. I think that makes such a difference, too.

Even though she has become very good at doing me orally, she was reluctant for many years for me to do her that way. During the last two decades or so, especially when she really gets excited, she has increasingly asked me to go down on her, which I absolutely love.

When I do go down, I not only love how she tastes and the perfume-like scent that fills my head with very enticing thoughts, but I especially like the way she moves her legs all over and massages the hair on my head, pushing my tongue and mouth harder and harder against her pubic area when she is reaching the point of no return. Then her legs invariably start shaking uncontrollably and she arches her back higher and higher against me. I guess I feel her orgasms more that way than when I am inside her, and it is very exciting for me to be right down there in the middle of the glorious action.

Anyway, she is truly amazing when she gets going. You asked for something surprising, and I'm sure this would probably surprise anyone who knows her—that she can be such a sex pistol when she lets go. To see her, sitting in church or talking with people, you'd probably never believe it. She looks like a petite little grandmother, which she is, but looks can be deceiving. In bed, and sometimes even before we make it to a bed, she's a feisty little vixen who knows exactly what I like. I love all these facets about her, especially that. And even though it's going to be changed a lot in your book, I'm glad that I finally get to say that.

THELMA

I'm still red-faced from hearing Chuck talk about me like that. I think he gives me too much credit. Actually, we were both pretty inexperienced when we got married, so we got to learn everything together. He is the best, most thoughtful teacher in the world, I believe. He has always been so patient and caring. And we've learned a lot together. And we feel that God has given us a lot of wisdom through the years in the way we treat each other.

He wasn't always so patient that way when it came to getting things done around the churches we served in—he was a hard-charger sometimes, always wanting to save the world and not understanding why everyone wasn't as dedicated as he was. But in bed he has always been such a good, patient, caring man. I was so young and trembling when we first had sex, and he could have reacted in ways that would have destroyed my trust in him. Even back then, and through the years, as well, he kept emphasizing how good I was, even when I wasn't so sure of myself, and it always made me want to please him even more.

Another thing that I appreciate so much about Chuck is that he could have been just like his father if he had wanted. Certainly there are men in the ministry—or any profession—who don't have as high of standards as Chuck does. He is breathtakingly handsome, the spitting image of his father, and so perfectly built. He looks like a million dollars in clothes—whether he is wearing a suit or a golf shirt and slacks. When he has no clothes on, he is even better looking. As he has gotten older, and the hair on his head, chest and below has turned mostly white, he is even sexier to me. I get aroused just thinking about it.

What I'm saying is that I'm sure he could have a different woman every day of the week, even now at 70 years old, but he chooses to be with me. That really makes me feel good about him and me, and it causes me to fall even more in love with him when I think about it.

It's no wonder that I get so excited about him, especially when I see him firing with both barrels from the pulpit. He is so suave and sensual to me as he glides from side to side, making points with his arms, sometimes charming people and sometimes stepping all over their toes, so to speak. He's always impeccably dressed and handsome. People absolutely love him as a preacher, and they always have. His voice is so deep and stirring. You can tell that he believes what he is saying to the core. And with all that he is and says, he touches me down to my toes.

Since the question relates to how people would be surprised, the point I'm getting to is that people would be surprised if they could see inside my mind when he preaches.

There are lots of times that I look at him in the pulpit and especially when he walks down from the platform close to where I'm sitting, that I can hardly restrain myself from staring at his pubic area. He has preferred to wear double-breasted suits for as long as I can remember, and there's something about the way the cloth from his coat sort of hides his wonderful private area from view. It simply makes me very excited. Maybe it's like the forbidden, hidden fruit, even though

I know I can see it and touch it later when we get home. I can't even explain it, but not being able to see under the front part of the suit jacket sometimes makes me very, very aroused, even after all these years.

When he walks close to me, I almost have to hold both my hands tightly to keep one from reaching up under his suit coat and touching his warm privates underneath. Now wouldn't that shock the church people? Imagine the local newspaper headlines after that!

This is embarrassing to admit, but since we've gone this far, and since our names and details will be changed, maybe this will help someone else out there who has the same feeling about love and marriage in that person's situation.

I'll give you an actual example that happened less than a month ago. We left a church after the Sunday night service and headed home, rather than staying over in a motel since we were less than two hours from our town.

We planned to stop at a restaurant near our home when we reached our city, so he still had his double-breasted suit on as we drove. I kept looking at him as we drove through the night. He was so handsome with his sharp tie, nice long legs under the steering wheel, shiny leather shoes covering his sexy feet. Yes, even his feet are sexy to me!

As I stared at him, I even thought about how sensual his hands were and even the little tufts of hair on his fingers. But my eyes kept going back to the area hidden underneath his suit where his beautiful sexual parts were.

Finally, I could stand it no longer. It was dark enough as we drove through the night that no one could see me, so I surprised both him AND me. I slid over, reached underneath the bottom of his suit, unbelted his trousers and unzipped his pants.

He laughed and asked me what I was doing. I told him to just enjoy himself and try not to run off the road. Then I pulled his growing penis through the opening on his underwear, leaned over and put as much of it as I could inside my mouth. I had never done it before from the side with him sitting up and driving, but I liked it. I especially liked what it was doing to him.

He told me later that he could hardly keep the car on the highway. I tried to make as much noise as possible, and I could tell that he was really enjoying it.

When he went off suddenly, it caught me by surprise, and even though he generally doesn't explode as much liquid now as he used to when he was younger, we ended up with some of his semen on my hair and coat, not to mention the fact that it sprayed over his suit coat and pants, too.

I loved it, for I knew that I had given him something unlike anything he had ever experienced before. And it was all my idea. I liked that, too. I especially enjoyed the fact that I surprised him so much.

He could hardly talk for awhile, and when he did, all he did was grin and keep saying "Thelma...Thelma" over and over and touching me. I loved that.

I didn't say anything, just leaned my head against his shoulder, and put my hand underneath his suit again to hold his wet penis in my hand. We drove all the way home that way without saying a word.

Obviously, we didn't make it to the restaurant. Thankfully, we could hit the remote control, drive into the garage and go right inside our home without having to worry about letting anybody see us in that condition, pants still unzipped and spots over his clothes and my hair.

And when we got home, watching him take off his suit, I got even more excited. He draped his clothes over a chair and went into the bathroom to get ready for bed. He doesn't even know this until now, but while he was in the bathroom, I went over and touched the material around the crotch of his pants that was still slightly wet. I even smelled it and touched it with my tongue. I did the same thing with the middle part of his double-breasted suit.

A couple of days later, I decided to surprise him again. While he was showering one morning, I took all my clothes off. When he emerged from the shower, I held one of his dress coats for him and asked him to put it on and button it. It was so exciting, since for the first time I could see his private parts actually hanging down below the front part of his double-breasted suit as I had fantasized in so many church services.

I knelt down in front of him, feeling him with both hands from the ankles up to his crotch. I could see him growing. Every time I saw him hanging longer and longer below the suit, it sent thunderbolts through me.

I asked him to leave the coat on, and I pulled him on top of me on the bed. By then, he could have done anything to me and I would have responded violently.

He did the best thing he could have done. He moved me so my bottom was at the edge of the bed, then he propped pillows underneath my bottom, stood over me, lifted both of my legs, eased in and then began plunging deep inside me.

With every stroke in and out, the front of his suit kept brushing against my pubic hair and my legs. I could see him standing over me, going in and out, with his double-breasted suit. I remember trying to look down at his crotch area, but by then he was moving faster and faster and all I could do was hang onto the suit lapels and feel him go off deep inside me. It was spectacular!

We've had sex several times since then with him in his double-breasted suit coat. I just love seeing him stiffen and lengthen, his beautifully shaped penis and testicles hanging down beneath his coat.

The last two times I even asked him to leave all his clothes on so I could feel underneath that front area of his coat and touch inside his trousers. I discovered that I even enjoyed going up the leg of his pants and feeling as high up his leg as I can with my hands. He really seems to like this when we do it with his suit on. I know I do!

I've gone on and on with this to the point that I must be boring you. Let me just finish this question by saying that people who know us would really be surprised if they knew some of the things we do, but they are our own private and wonderful things, and I certainly don't see anything wrong with them. I look forward to finding new ways to please him, and I'm more excited than ever as he finds ways to please me.

(5) In your opinion, what is the secret to being a seasoned, sensual senior, and what is one story you would like to tell that would help people understand how special sex can be to people over 60?

CHUCK

Sex is so much more than the sexual act. I've worked with enough people to know that people lose interest in sex often at the same time that they lose their zest for life. I've heard it said before that you don't stop having sex because you grow old, but you grow old because you stop having sex. The more birthday candles I have to blow out each year, the more I believe the truth in that statement.

People who are active and giving and alive in other areas of their lives just naturally seem to keep active in their sex lives. It almost always goes together, from what I've seen.

THELMA

What Chuck says is so true. I've seen people who are 40 or 50 and have become old and shriveled and selfish. It almost always seems like they give up on having satisfied sexual lives at the same time they give up on being happy in other areas.

At the same time, there are people who keep young and active long after they get old in years. My parents passed away last year, both in their nineties, and my mother confessed to me not long before she died that one of the greatest memories she had was that my father and her had such a good time "peeling his cucumber," as she called it, on her ninetieth birthday. I was shocked when she talked so openly. I was even more shocked later when he patted Mother's leg and called her his "Red Hot Mama." There are some things you just never think you'll hear from your parents.

I was embarrassed then and didn't know what to say, but I sometimes wish I would have made a bigger thing about how happy I was that they still enjoyed each other so much.

I want to be like that with Chuck. If we live to be 120, I want us to keep doing it in one way or another. And yes, I hope he keeps wearing double-breasted suits forever!

FRANCO (74)
STUDENT & MENTOR

"I was successful because I helped women become very good at lovemaking. They always thought I was the great lover, but actually I was just a good teacher. They became good lovers; I simply got to enjoy what I helped create."

—FRANCO

A NOTE FROM THE EDITORS: One of the over-riding purposes of this book has been to promote long-term relationships, ideally with a monogamous relationship in the bonds of marriage. Franco's story, as you will read, contains some shocking and intimate details about his past that definitely do not promote these values. However, the concepts he discussed during several interviews about romance and keeping the relationship vibrant are among the best we have seen. We have included it for your education and benefit, but we offer this cautionary warning that it contains rather graphic details and unusual situations. If these disturb you, please skip to Chapter 10.

(1) What is your age, background and general health?

I am 74, born in France, but have lived all over the world. My father was part French, Greek and Italian, and my mother was from Spain, so I grew up knowing four languages naturally. I soon learned English, too, since we lived in a resort area that catered to wealthy Britons and Americans, and to a lesser extent to people from throughout Europe, Africa and Asia.

What I'm going to say about myself is something that I would only say because two of my dearest friends trust you implicitly. Plus, you have promised complete anonymity, which is the only way I would do this.

I have been encouraged for many years to write a book, and I've been approached several times about working with a screenwriter on a film. I simply don't want the hassles and don't need the money.

Plus, there are some well-known people with whom I have been associated whose families are still living. I don't want them as enemies. So this interview, perhaps, is my way to explain a bit about my past without having the negative aspects. It lets me share some things without subjecting myself to anything detrimental.

Here's the deep-dark secret that few people alive today know: I spent many years of my life as a gigolo.

I don't know how else to say it and you can do whatever you want in the published interview. My parents were very poor during my childhood. Poverty affects different people differently. I was the oldest of nine brothers and sisters, and most of them reacted by working very hard at trades like my parents, even though it meant remaining in the lower class. I was eventually able to help three of my youngest siblings to be educated at the university, and they have lived very well, as have my other brothers and sisters.

As for myself, even as a child I decided that I would do whatever it took to escape the poverty and live like the elite, once I saw how they lived. I am grateful that I wasn't sold into slavery, as some boys and girls of other parents were, and that I was guided very carefully by a family member to learn my craft well.

I am no longer a gigolo. With all the diseases today, I don't want to risk myself anymore. I'm not particularly proud of what I did during those years, but I'm glad that I am still going strong and am healthy after all these years.

You asked about my health. I've always been trim, and I'm proud of the fact that I weigh what I did at 30. I drink a little glass of French burgundy every day, but not too much. I walk and swim and bike as much as I can, and I do strength training and stretching every single day. I believe in the value of vitamin D, so I have a special private place beside my pool where I can lay in the sun nude nearly every day of the year for 20 to 30 minutes or more. I make sure I take Omega 3 and a multi-vitamin and mineral supplement every day. I also take a several all-natural supplements that are especially suited to an older male's health and sexuality.

I have a masseuse who comes twice a week to help keep me limber and stretched. I eat well, but sparingly. And my great pursuit, most of my life, has been the good life. That has never changed.

(2) Is sex still a part of your life, and, if so, how has it (and you) changed over the years?

Sex has always been part of my life, from the time I was a young boy of nine. The wealthy Europeans, Britons, Americans, Asians and Africans who visited my country, I discovered, were sometimes very decadent. I was used as a sex toy by men, women and sometimes couples, sometimes even several couples at one time.

I didn't understand it. I just took it as something relatively normal for a boy in that lifestyle. This was long before I could enjoy sex myself, in the true sense, so it was just for the money for my poverty-stricken family.

My parents never knew. Everything was arranged for me by my Uncle Rafael who worked at one of the best resorts near the sea. My parents were told by Rafael that he wanted me to learn a trade at the resort. He told them through the next few years that I was a very good general helper, and they either bought that idea or knew more that they let on and merely looked the other way. Anyway, from the time I was nine, I lived at the hotel resort, and my uncle sent money each week to my parents.

Uncle Rafael told my parents that he picked me because I was strong and reliable and would be good to help take care of the resort's grounds. But the very first day, he took me aside and told me that he picked me because I was the most handsome boy he had ever seen. It was true. I look at the pictures of me then, and I was a beautiful youngster with the fairest skin, the darkest hair and the biggest, most innocent eyes you ever saw. I was built well, even then, so I always looked good in whatever clothing I wore.

I didn't stay innocent for long. From that point I spent a lot of time with my clothing off in the suites of some of the richest people who visited the South of France. Some of the things I did were unspeakable and painful, and some of them were merely unpleasant. On the other hand, some were actually pleasurable for me, even before I reached puberty.

It was demeaning, of course, to simply grab my ankles and feel a man fumble around until he got inside me, then feeling the stokes and hearing the heavy breathing until he went off. Almost always, as soon as it was over, I was quickly told to leave the room. Some men were a little more affectionate, touching and caressing me all over. Almost all of the women were much more tender toward me, with a few notable exceptions that I'd like to forget.

My uncle always took care of the arrangements and payments during those early years, so I was mostly concerned with staying well-groomed, polite and obliging in the most intimate ways.

Frankly, after I realized what was going on, I loved the attention, even when I was with boorish or disgusting people. When I was with people who were more kindhearted and civilized, I really enjoyed both the interest and occasional affection.

Once I reached puberty, my clientele changed, since I was no longer a little doe-eyed, dark-haired boy that both the men and women liked fondling and using somewhat as a toy. Instead of peach fuzz and smallness, I started getting dark hair on my body and more adult-looking features and genitalia. I became a very good kisser, and enjoyed what my kisses did when I applied them very skillfully, especially to the women.

There were still a few men who wanted an innocent-looking young teenage male, but I really didn't enjoy the time with them. I also did it sometimes, even after puberty, with couples, but it wasn't my favorite thing to do. I didn't particularly care for the smell of most men, nor did I enjoy it when their semen splashed over me or in me.

I always thought that most men were uncouth and boorish. After the sex act was over, as mentioned before, they often wanted me out of the room as soon as possible, as if they were suddenly guilty for what they had just done, and, I suppose, I was an obvious reminder. The women, on the other hand, liked for me to stay with them, to touch, hold and kiss them for awhile, sometimes throughout the night.

But even with the men, I didn't say anything, of course. I did what they wanted. The more pleasure I gave, the more money and tips they left with Raphael.

That went on until I was 14 or 15. By then I had developed a distinct taste for women, so I told Rafael that I only wanted to go with women. Sometimes he still had me go with couples, but it was mostly with the rich men who enjoyed getting their jollies by watching a young man do it with their women. Almost always, they would sit or lie beside us so they could see the stroking in and out from up-close, but I'm not sure if they liked seeing my genitals or the female sexual parts. Probably the combination. I didn't care. The money was almost always superb when it involved very rich couples who were willing to pay to do anything they wanted, especially if they were international celebrities or the inevitable *noveau riche* who were excited about something that seemed so Old Worldish and taboo.

It was the women that I enjoyed (and the money, of course). And lots of women, I discovered, enjoyed romping around the bedroom with a handsome, young, dark-haired French teenager who could make them feel young again. Almost all of them talked about my kisses, and they liked lots of different kinds of fondling. They liked my caresses before, during and after the sex act.

I was often told by the women that most men weren't very good kissers. I had experienced that firsthand, myself, so I decided to focus on becoming one of the best kissers. As I got older and my body changed, I knew by seeing, touching and giving pleasure to enough penises up close that I was pretty well endowed, but not as large as *le verge en érection* I had seen before. Still, I learned that size was definitely not everything, and I became very motivated to become the most skilled kisser and lover as I could be.

This knowledge and desire was hardly unselfish. It was quite self-serving, for I discovered that the clients would shower me with gifts and money when I did especially well, especially the ones who were somewhat older or less beautiful.

Uncle Rafael still worked as a gigolo himself, even though by then he had taken a wife and had several children by then. He taught me lots of ways to make more money. He never actually had sex with me, but he would mainly talk to me and help me understand how to use my talents better and better. There were many times Rafael even had me sit in a closet and watch him in action with a wealthy woman, a man or couple. He was truly a master with his body, and could do extraordinary things with his tongue and mouth. During intercourse, he would sometimes look over and secretly wink at me where I was hiding.

He was well-endowed, but he certainly didn't have the longest or largest tool I had ever seen. Still, he sure knew how to use his entire body as a finely-tuned instrument. He could literally make both men and women pant and beg for more, that's how good he was.

I was always amazed at how much control he had over the situation and himself, and I determined to become a masterful lover like my uncle.

Once in awhile, if some rich woman wanted it and was willing to pay a lot of extra money, Rafael and I even did it to the same woman at the same time. I didn't really like it that way, probably because I had developed a pretty big ego by then, and I didn't like to be compared so closely to Rafael who was truly an accomplished lover.

Mostly, we worked independently. Eventually he had several other young men who worked as gigolos there at the resort, but my uncle and I were the highest paid of all, and both of us had clients who came to visit regularly from quite a few places around the world, including America, Africa, and Asia—many of them household names that included politicians, musicians, film stars, and certainly financial tycoons. The one constant was that they all had to be pretty well off to stay at the resort and rather brazen or needy to employ a gigolo.

There were numerous young ladies who worked at the resort as highly paid call girls, but that was controlled by one of the families in that region. Rafael had nothing to do with that part of the business, or at least I don't think he did.

Rafael became very wealthy and lived extremely well until he somehow became involved in the throes of the Cold War. He was killed, apparently by communist agents from either Italy or Soviet Russia. I was never able to find out exactly what happened, and I was told in no uncertain terms by very powerful people that I should stop trying to uncover more details.

I was saddened, of course, by the turn of events, but believe me, there were women on both sides of the Atlantic Ocean who wept with great remorse when they heard about Rafael's death. I knew because I met some of them later. They missed him immensely. Thankfully, they were quite willing to pay well for a younger version who bore a strikingly similar appearance, both clothed and unclothed, to their older, favorite, now-departed lover.

Being around Rafael was like apprenticing with a master gigolo. There apparently weren't that many good ones, even in the South of France or other parts of Europe, so the better I became, the more money I could make. The more money I made, the more money it meant for myself and my family.

Rafael had been very fair to me and kept a lot of money stashed away for me that he didn't tell my parents about. I didn't learn about that until after he was gone.

Since that time, I've used what my uncle taught me, as well as what I discovered myself, to make some of the wealthiest and famous women in the world satisfied. I haven't worked as a gigolo for years, but only during the past five years have I thought of staying with one woman and maybe even having a child or two to carry on my name.

I no longer need the money. As mentioned, my uncle secretly invested a lot of money in my name, and after his untimely demise, I was contacted by one of his business partners who explained that I had a considerable sum available when I wanted it.

Then a couple of years after Rafael's murder, I decided to go to America. I lived in a New York City townhouse for awhile with one elderly couple I had known intimately while still in France. She was a young thing, maybe 15 or 16 when she and her 80-year-old beau met my uncle.

By the time I began spending time with them, they had been married for a few years. Not long afterward, I moved to New York to a mostly exclusively arrangement with them. Plus, after what happened to my uncle, I was aware that whatever had happened to him could easily happen to me.

I thoroughly enjoyed America, though my relationship with the New York couple was rather unusual. The only way I know to describe it is to tell you exactly the way it was, then you can edit out what you think is simply too much information.

Let's just say that the elderly husband had a thing for touching my buttocks, inner thighs and genitals while I caressed his wife all over and made love to her. He also enjoyed touching her all over while it was happening.

He never seemed to want sex himself, but just enjoyed looking at what was happening and touching me, and he especially liked it the more drenched I became from stroking his wife's vagina.

To this day, I don't know if he was homosexual, bi-sexual, asexual or merely trying to re-live his youth through me. All I know is that he wasn't a casual observer. He really got into it and seemed to get even more excited when his wife climaxed vigorously. His face would redden and he would touch me more passionately, but he never seemed to want anything himself. He really liked to touch his wife's wet pubic area and my genitals after we were finished. Sometimes he seemed to like to stick a finger inside his wife, then other times he would focus more on stroking me, then rubbing the wetness all over her and me.

I often lay there between him and her while he touched me and her, long after we were finished. Sometimes I would even get aroused again as he fondled and rubbed me against his wife's labia. There were many times that I ejaculated again all over his hands as he stroked me.

It was always strange to me that he never seemed to want anything himself. Every time, he would eventually fall asleep, and his wife would tap me quietly and motion for me to kiss her one more time and leave. We did it that way with little variation hundreds of times during the four years I lived with them.

I never quite understood what he was doing. Or why? Out of appreciation for being very well-paid, I suppose, there were numerous times I turned to him after finishing with her, reaching out to touch him and letting him know openly that I would do whatever he expected me to. He always seemed to want me to do more, but then would shake his head and wave me off, sometimes rather indignantly, as though I had insulted him. But the next time he would be back for more of the same.

Maybe he did it to himself later or did it with her after I left their bedroom. Maybe he simply didn't have fire left in the engine room. I don't know, since I never saw him undressed even once. He never explained why he did what he did, nor did his wife. After awhile I figured that it didn't matter much as long as they got what they wanted and paid me extremely well.

There were few words ever spoken in their *boudoir*, but they did talk openly to me outside the bedroom. In time, we became very close. I listened a lot, especially when they shared anything about business.

He had children and grandchildren from a previous marriage, but they all lived out in California. Some of the family members were involved as owners in one of the large motion picture studios. I don't know if there was bad blood involved, or if they didn't like the patriarch's young wife, but all I know is that their family never came around, and the couple seldom ever went out West to see them.

As for me, I think they just liked having someone around to talk to as much as the sexual part, strange as it was. So I became his "nephew from Europe" and lived with them for four years. They actually introduced me that way. They taught me how to dress like the upper classes of New York, and how to stand and sit and talk in a way that would have made George Bernard Shaw proud. I learned the importance of books and logic from them, spending hundreds of hours in their massive library. I also started spreading out, making life a little sweeter for several other high society's *grande dames* and *la beau monde*, all with their full knowledge and encouragement.

My benefactors died in a tragic airplane crash, ironically on their way to begin rebuilding fences with the West Coast family members. Sad as it was for me, their departure, after probate, left me with a nice house on Long Island, an even nicer nest egg in the bank, and most of their library.

The best thing they did, however, was to give me an education. Plus, they introduced me to a number of their business associates and taught me the ropes of investing and economics. I gave them a lot of enjoyment, I suppose, but I got even more. They were my *entree* to American power and wealth.

Even though I continued working, so to speak, I also invested heavily in the stock market and real estate during the next decades. I am a millionaire many times over and could have stopped hustling the wealthy decades ago, but I simply enjoyed making love with beautiful, powerful and rich women. I won't tell you any specifics about them, since privacy was always one of my most ironclad rules, but you would recognize many names, although the best ones were generally the most private and unrecognized people. It's not that I'm specifically proud of bedding them, but it was my job for many years—what I liked to do—and I was very good at it.

I haven't been a gigolo in the strictest sense since the mid-Seventies. My pay became the information they provided—from stock information and impending trades to major real estate deals their husbands were involved with. Plus, I always received expensive gifts from women who simply enjoyed my skills. Sometimes their husbands knew what was going on, and sometimes not. Frankly, I didn't care, as long as the "rules of engagement," whatever that entailed, were followed astutely.

I gave my clients what they wanted—discreet romance, and they gave me what I wanted—a gateway to the most privileged information that made me increasingly wealthy and financially independent. It worked very well for everyone involved.

The only reason I would participate in something like this study is that my future wife wants me to, even though she doesn't want to go through an interview herself. And maybe I feel I can help men become better lovers so their women don't have to look elsewhere for people like me.

I suppose it seems strange for me to say this, but I do believe in marriage and families, and I really believe that old-fashioned morals and honesty are the best things between men and women. It's just that I never lived by those rules from the time I was nine until recently. I'm committed to being successful in my upcoming marriage, and I know first-hand the perils of playing around. As I say these things, I realize that I've changed more than I would have previously admitted.

(3) If you are currently involved in an intimate relationship, how long has it lasted? What has made it last? What have been the best (or worse) parts of the relationship?

For the past two years, I have been involved with a wonderful woman who is in her thirties. She is brilliant, has a master's degree in international relations from a well-respected university, and is currently working on her doctorate at an ivy-league college. We met through an event she was hosting, ended up talking for hours afterward, and before long both of us fell headlong in love—quite unexpectedly.

Believe it or not, we haven't yet made love, though we have been quite involved romantically. She is very particular about her standards, and I love her enough to respect her beliefs. We are getting married in a few months. We may even try to have a child or two in the next few years. I can afford a family, of course, and I'm not fearful of starting one, even though I am in my seventies. I think I could be a very good father, if for no other reason than to avoid the loneliness and pain I often felt as a child.

I had a vasectomy many years ago, but thankfully I have enough frozen sperm waiting to get my future wife pregnant as many times as she wants. My only hesitation is that if I die within the next decade or two, who would be there to be a father to the children? They would be taken care of financially, but there are more important things than money. Those things still cause me great concern, and I won't go ahead with plans for a family unless I feel peace about it first. My fiancé is willing to accept my decision, whether we will have children or not.

(4) What details about you, your partner and your relationship would surprise people if they knew?

I am going to answer this in terms of my current partner and the life I want to build with her. We are committed to be faithful exclusively to each other. In that sense, I have truly turned over a new leaf, so to speak.

So to answer your question, probably the most surprising thing to friends who knew me before is that I am truly in the process of becoming a family man.

Some people from the old days wouldn't believe that in a million years.

And I think the other surprising thing is how much I could teach them to become better lovers. Maybe that's the reason that I'm doing this interview—to share very simple steps to becoming a masterful and romantic man.

If there is a secret, I believe it's the fact that I have learned how to read a woman very well. I can read men, too, but since I was never interested in romance with them, I always focused on the women.

As such, if men only knew how simple romance really is, there would be little need for gigolos or prostitution or cheating. Real romance is built on several simple principles:.

NOTE FROM THE EDITORS: These nine principles were given in bits and pieces during two separate interviews with Franco. Because they are so insightful and relevant to the stated purpose of this book, we have attempted to reorganize and rewrite them in a condensed, orderly form for your benefit.

These key points are specifically for men, but there may be some things women find helpful, as well.

FIRST, focus all your attention on your lover until you can see clear through to her soul. Women are complex and sometimes elusive, but if you try, you can learn so much about them by talking with them and looking into their eyes as you listen.

When you touch a woman, watch how she responds and learn from it. Every woman has her own special places that she likes to be kissed and stroked and nuzzled. If you want to please her, determine to learn as much as you can about her.

Very few men ever do this one thing that will revolutionize your relationship. I have no idea why.

SECONDLY, learn how to use the information you discover to give her lots of pleasure. Most men focus on their own pleasure. Do it differently and you will separate yourself from most men. Focus on her pleasure.

Appeal to all her senses as you give her pleasure. Flowers are wonderfully sensuous because of their beauty, their fragrance and their texture. You can never go wrong with flowers, unless she is allergic to them, of course!

Develop your own personal and well-stocked tool chest of scented oils, beautiful candles, fragrant incense, pleasure-giving vibrators and dildos, feathers and other play-things. Certain cultures are better at this than others—notably the French, Italians, Greek and Chinese.

Yet at the same time you should never use "tools" to take place of tenderness.

And I'm especially adamant that you should never use anything that causes pain—things such as whips, extreme penis extenders and domination devices. I also don't like pornography. I simply don't like anything that hurts people or shows disrespect to women.

Mainly, keep it simple, but show that you are concerned about her pleasure. Not every woman likes every single "tool" that you come up with, but if you focus on what she likes, you will make her feel very important and cherished.

Most men show up with a hopefully erect penis and a smile. You can separate yourself from those other men by becoming *le ouvrier*, an artisan. A great *artiste* uses only what he needs to paint or sculpt a masterpiece—no more and certainly no less. You can learn to do the same thing. Simplicity is always the highest form of elegance, in life and definitely in romance.

THIRDLY, use the information you learn to teach her how to grow and develop as a lover, to be *eleve d'amour*, a student of love. As you encourage and teach her to know what makes a man respond, you build her confidence. Many women aren't very confident, and when you help a woman become confident, you unleash something wonderful.

FOURTH, and this is one of the most important, don't concentrate on intercourse. Be different from the typical guy who has only one goal and races toward it, ignoring the wonderful scenery and sensory experiences along the way. Do the right things that offer her pleasure, then intercourse and orgasms will take care of themselves when the time is right.

Instead of intercourse, focus on foreplay and after play. Most men are so concerned with their size and their technique and their orgasm, and they miss the whole point. Women want companionship and love and touching and kissing, not mere sex. Frankly, they don't give a damn about size or what stroke or position you employ, as long as you are sensual.

Instead of going directly for the clitoris and vagina, concentrate delicately and deliciously on the other erogenous zones—her feet, wrists, nipples, ears, nape of the neck, small of the back, buttocks, behind the knees, inner thighs and certainly her lips. With practice, she will gladly tell you what she especially enjoys.

If men could only understand the importance of foreplay and after play, they would discover that their women would worship them.

In fact, I believe that after play is incredibly vital, perhaps more important than what happens before and during intercourse.

After play is the often-neglected, flower-strewn path that leads you directly back to the front gate of her sexual garden. The more you invest in her pleasure, especially after the climax, the more open and delicious the front garden gate becomes.

FIFTH, any good lover learns a few techniques that allow him to enter his woman whether he is particularly hard or not. I say that because one of the reasons most men don't take more time for more foreplay is their often-real fear that they can't keep an erection going indefinitely until the woman is ready and willing. But many times you must.

I learned a long time ago from Uncle Rafael that a full erection is not necessary for sex, and if you are concentrating on your woman's pleasure, your tool may sometimes become stiff, then relax, going up and down perhaps a few times before you decide to make your *accès magnifique*. You may also get more or less rigid even inside her, depending upon how long you desire to go and what other activities you are doing elsewhere on her body.

Often, when I brought a woman to her peak with my fingers or mouth or vibrator, I learned to time things so I got erect and ready to go inside right after she had a clitoral orgasm. But if she took longer than I planned or if I got softer than I would like, I simply learned to make sure I was well lubricated, then had her lay on her back with her right leg up. I lay beside her, approached her crossways, scooting up from beneath her, with my upper torso to her right. I'd put my right leg over her left leg, and my left leg underneath her, basically with my two legs "scissoring" her left leg. It was always relatively easy to get my penis inside her that way, even if it wasn't solid as a rock, especially when I lubricated her and myself well. A few strokes, especially if she touched my scrotum at the same time, and I'd be poised for action as long as I wanted to go with both of us in a very relaxed position.

Any man can do that position with a little practice and a willing partner, especially since his weight isn't on her and he is free to explore her most tantalizing areas as he moves in and out of her.

Another wonderful way to go inside, whether you have a full erection or not, is to prop a few pillows on the edge of the bed, then lay her down on her back with her buttocks on the pillows, high enough to be at the same height as your penis. Stand up and approach her after lubricating yourself well. Lift her legs up and slide yourself in with your hand, then as you get harder, you can start to stroke at will.

Again, if you have trouble getting it up either scissoring it or from the edge of the bed, you can encourage her to reach around and touch your scrotum and buttocks. *Merci!* That one works like a charm. If you are standing up and she is on the edge of the bed, you have to lift your right leg and put your foot on the bed for her to be able to reach underneath and touch your scrotum and inner thighs, but it works amazingly well.

It takes a little practice, but these two positions take all the pressure off of getting an erection and being able to perform. Then you can enjoy foreplay as long as you and your partner desire, then you can get it up when you are ready.

Another thing to remember is that sex doesn't have to end in an erection and intercourse. Most Western cultures believe that, but it is not always true.

Many times I've had women from many different cultures who told me that they didn't want me to penetrate them, but only wanted me to hold them close. Men generally don't like that idea, but if you can accept the concept and are willing to be loving, rather than just making love, you will be more able to accept the times your penis doesn't respond like a charging *toro*.

SIXTH, learn how to avoid ejaculating before you choose to let it go. Women almost always want intercourse longer than men, so it is important to learn how to go as long as you desire. In fact, it's one of the clear skills of a masterful lover.

Again, Rafael was a virtuoso at this.

"There's a magic line," he used to say, "and the masterful lover decides when and how to cross it."

After I reached puberty and started having ejaculations, he taught me to reach my peak without actually going over the edge. I got good enough that I could feel most of the feelings of ejaculation, but could keep from actually releasing my semen.

I reached the point that I could usually go almost as long as I wanted. After awhile, of course, the pressure builds up to the point that no one can stop it, but the better you get at controlling it, the more pleasure you can give to the woman. And there is nothing more exciting than tantalizing a woman until she actually begins imploring and begging for her final climax.

Rafael taught me how to stop when I was getting too close by spending time kissing and fondling with the penis as deep as possible and moving very little inside her.

He even had a technique where he would stop, as deeply as possible inside her, then he would reach down with a thumb and forefinger to gently squeeze his penis at the base of his shaft. For some reason, after applying a little pressure for a moment, he could usually go on indefinitely.

Rafael even taught me to control my ejaculation by mentally practicing English, Latin or doing mathematics—anything to keep my mind off the growing need to erupt. I didn't like that technique as well as simply stroking and caressing on my partner, focusing on her body and desires, watching her building to the point of no return.

Once you get skillful at controlling your ejaculation, you can move onto giving a woman whatever she wants—fast strokes, slow movement, longer strokes, deep twitches or whatever combination suits your fancy. Variety really is the spice of life, especially when it comes to stroking inside a woman.

Sometimes I even found it effective to vary the speed of my stroke as I went in and out, especially when I pulled outward slowly, then quickly went in, then kept repeating this slow-fast stroke until the pressure builds to the point that you can't hold back any longer. Often that tantalizing pattern leaves a woman breathing in time to your strokes, then eventually begging you to finish her quickly.

I found that every woman in the world, regardless of background or experience, loves to be able to trust you enough to let you know what she wants. That only happens if you let her know that your main goal is to give her pleasure. Sometimes, it just takes a little encouragement on your part to get her to express herself.

To control the tempo, you must be in control. There is no more pleasurable sex than after a woman has several orgasms and finally reaches such a point of desire that she begins pleading with you to explode inside her and finish her off. What a rush! She thinks you are Superman, and you feel like the Man of Steel, too, *sans* tights and cape.

SEVENTH, knowing a few foreign languages can help, too, for women love it when you talk to them in French or Russian or Italian or Spanish—something other than what they are. Although it is very unusual, I have actually had a few women who could reach their peak during foreplay without me inside them or touching their love flesh, simply by having me nibble their necks and murmuring—in French or Italian or Swahili—how wonderful, beautiful and sensual they were.

When I saw my Uncle Rafael do this the first time, as I hid in the closet watching him in action, I was utterly amazed. He had been involved in heavy foreplay with an African woman for some time, yet he had purposely not touched the woman's clitoris. He was stroking her with his hands, nuzzling her neck, and then he began using several Italian phrases. Though he hadn't touched her clitoris or gone inside her yet, at the romantic sound of a foreign language and with his breaths on her neck, the woman's entire body began quaking and her breaths quickened until she began to shriek.

Not long afterward, he did the same thing with an Italian countess, this time speaking to her in the most earthy Portuguese dialect at the right moment. Different woman, different language, same erotic result. He always picked a language that was foreign to that particular woman.

From the first time I saw him do this, I was so impressed and made up my mind right then to add as many amorous foreign phrases as I could learn.

It didn't always work as well with me as with Rafael, but I found that whether you can cause earth-shattering climaxes without touching a woman's love flesh, or whether you merely use it as a subtle enhancement along with everything else you do, I have yet to find a women who doesn't love it when you speak lovingly in a language that is foreign to her own, especially when it is one of the romantic languages, and most especially when you whisper it in her ear as both of you reach your peak and you deliver your *coup de grace*.

And while I'm on the subject, many women love classical music. Most men like rock music or Big Band or American country, but many women of good taste also enjoy being romanced with something very romantic and symphonic. I often use Strauss or Debussy or Chopin, but I might just as easily choose Glenn Miller or John Coltrane or even some avant-garde Brazilian jazz like Hermeto Pascoal e Grupo. For a very special occasion with a woman of great sophistication, I have been known to play violinist extraordinaire Efrem Zimbalist's "Petite Sérénade" with wonderful effects.

Until you experience it again and again, you won't believe how women respond remarkably and passionately to romantic music that you have thoughtfully selected, especially when you light candles around the room and murmur a few foreign phrases that fit the music at the appropriate moments. Then it becomes more than love-making. It becomes l`affaire d`amour.

EIGHTH, become a masterful kisser. I am one of the few people who has been kissed by men as well as watching them kissing up-close. I can tell you without reservation that most men are absolutely uncouth when it comes to kissing. They either smash against the partner's mouth, choke with their tongue or merely peck in a disinterested way. Women absolutely love a man who uses his mouth, nose, chin and tongue as finely tuned instruments. I've actually seen men tongue women as if they were trying to ream the woman's mouth out or to touch her tonsils. Non! Women want gentleness. They want

tenderness. They want temptation and titil-
lation. They want you to electrify and excite
them.

Granted, I was well-paid, but as I mentioned before in an earlier discussion of a
woman's erogenous zones, I learned many
secrets of sensuality by spending hours in
foreplay, kissing all over her face, her eye-
brows, her temples, the lobes of her ears, all
over her neck, her shoulders, the small of
her back, the inside of her knees, her ankles,
her fingers, and on some women, even her
underarms. A darting tongue in all of those
erogenous places works magic, too. The combination often drives a woman into frenzy. No
matter what you do from that point, you can't
go wrong.

Sadly, most men after a few perfunc-
tory and tasteless kisses, then go right for
the woman's nipples, clitoris and into the
vagina—the Big Three. Boom! Boom! Boom!
And it's over. Or as the Americans sometimes
say, "Wham! Bam! Thank you, Ma'am!" That's
a big mistake, and a very, very, very common
one.

I learned to emphasize all the other things,
then when I finally got to the Big Three, the
woman always thought I was the best lover in
the world because she was so ready and willing. When you do this, the actual sex act is

icing on the cake, or maybe icing IN the cake. And a sweet, decadent cake and icing it can be if you do it right!

NINTH, and finally, become a good dancer. Nearly every woman I have romanced loves a man who can take her in his arms and move her gracefully around the room. Most men intuitively know this, but they aren't willing to do what it takes to learn how. Given the chance, a woman will often go to bed with an ugly old impoverished man who knows how to dance gracefully than with a younger, more handsome, richer man with two left feet or a lack of confidence on the dance floor.

The secret is in the way you romance a woman while you dance, not just the technique of moving around the floor. Uncle Rafael told me that I should imagine a woman's vagina closed tightly when I first started dancing with her, then to imagine how that vagina opens more and more, naturally and wonderfully, just like the dewy petals of a blossoming rose, as I move her around the room. Just thinking about a woman's beautiful vagina getting more moist and opening up for my shaft always did wonders for me. It certainly made the dance more fun. As your hands and body caress each other, the ardor continues to grow to an intense heat.

We all knew this even as peach-fuzz faced boys trying to keep the hormones from racing to a boil-over point, but it becomes easy to neglect this magic secret as we get older.

The young males also often do something naturally than an older man forgets. As you dance, don't forget that holding a woman close, especially as you tastefully and occasionally touch the small of her back, can cause a very nice response. I've mentioned the erogenous zones. The small of the back is too often neglected, and if you are in a private place, dancing with increasingly daring placement of your hands as you dance can work wonders.

Lots of times, especially in the privacy of a *boudoir*, I have danced with women until I've had them drop to their knees and begin pulling my clothes off. It wasn't me—it was the dance.

I've had them stop dancing to push me onto the bed, unwilling to wait any longer. Seldom have I danced long with a woman whose panties aren't soaked delectably by the time we actually have sex. What a powerful aphrodisiac it is to feel and see the obvious, luscious results of a woman's growing ardor, a not-so-secret and moist signal that beckons you as a man to enter and begin the passionate parade of movements that lead to that moment of majestic fireworks.

What I am saying is that it is not just polished skills that causes the magic of intimacy and desire. It is how wonderfully well the human body and mind work to get us ready for lovemaking. And there is simply something erotic about dancing, especially when you do it tenderly and gracefully, that makes a woman appreciate you more as a man, and it makes them more than ready to open their "rose petals" to your growing *rapier*. Few men really understand and appreciate this. If they did, it would not only change their lives, but it would cause their lovemaking skills to explode dramatically.

So, there you have it—much of what I learned from my Uncle Rafael and years of pleasing many of the world's wealthiest women. There are other things, of course, but you don't really think that I will give all my secrets away, do you?

I apologize if said too much or explained it in any way to embarrass the person who eventually reads this interview. All I know is that I am passionate in the fact that if a man can become skillful at focusing on giving a woman pleasure, he will be a cherished partner for life.

Focusing on a woman means centering everything you do and think and say on her.

You become a detective. Once you do the first part, then the second part is fairly easy. In other words, you find out what she likes, then give her what she wants.

Many women are very insecure about romance and lovemaking. They see the great screen stories and read the novels, but very few of them feel as if they will ever experience that much love. I was successful because I helped women become very good lovers. They always thought I was a great lover, but actually I was just a good listener and teacher. They became the good lovers, and I got to enjoy what I helped create.

There have been times I have taken on women who had nothing but money, and little else, just to see if my theories really worked. One of my most successful Eliza Doolittles was during the mid-eighties with the young wife of a fabulously wealthy real estate tycoon. I will call them Joe and Helena. When I say "wealthy," I mean that Joe pissed away more money every month than you or I will ever make—combined. He had pursued Helena all over Europe, and had finally won her away from a German baron. She was such a diamond in the rough, extremely young and inexperienced, but he was a hard-charger and had no idea how to help her become a wonderful, satisfied wife and lover.

Joe bought Helena everything she wanted. He hired the best help. When they had children, he sent them to the finest schools. He lavished her with gifts and property. But when I met her, she was the loneliest, unhappiest 40-year-old I had ever seen. She had been beautiful once, but had become rather dowdy and even unattractive. She knew he was cheating on her, but she had become so unsure of herself and aware that she no longer had youthful beauty on her side. I think she had decided, by then, that security with her philandering husband was better than being branded in the society pages as his EX-wife.

I decided to take her on as a project. It took me two months to work my way into her life to the point that she would trust me. It took another month to work my way inside her very expensive underwear. The first time I went inside her, she was absolutely the worst lover I had been with, much like a stiff actor trying to enjoy something that she so obviously hated, even down to the forced sounds she made that revealed how unschooled and unnatural a lover she was. She desperately wanted to enjoy being womanly and making love, but she didn't know how. Therefore, everything was overdone and deliberate, even melodramatic, much like a very bad actress in an even worse porno movie. It took nearly three years to help transform her from a dowdy, middle-aged matron with no sense of spontaneous lovemaking skills into a lively, beautiful, naturally passionate and mature woman. Her wealth never changed significantly during that time. The only change was inside her.

I wasn't particularly attracted to her in a physical way. She didn't have a great figure. Her breasts and nose were much too perfectly sculpted by one of the world's finest cosmetic surgeons. Her hair, no matter how she coiffed it, was simply atrocious and overdone. As I said before, she wasn't good in bed. I wondered sometimes whether I could help her change.

What I concentrated on was Helena's skin. I know this sounds strange, but she had the most beautiful, sensuous skin. It didn't matter which cheek you were looking at—facial or backside—she had the most beautiful peaches-and-cream skin that you could imagine. The problem was that she didn't take very good care of herself because she was so busy playing the role that she felt was expected of her. I focused on her skin and gave her massages that lasted for hours using the richest of oils. I actually grew to love kissing and caressing her skin, especially her inner thighs. I told her over and over again how much I loved touching and looking at her skin.

The more I talked about her beautiful skin, and the more I stroked it and spent time in foreplay and after play, the more she responded to me when we actually made love. She started taking better care of herself in other ways, too, buying attractive clothing that worked well with her skin, not the old drab colors. I got her to color her hair differently and have it fixed in a way that would highlight her face.

She and I both knew that our relationship was temporary. There was no way she was going to leave her husband for me, and—though I never told her—there was no way I wanted to be involved with all the publicity that would happen if she did leave him. She simply trusted me and enjoyed all my encouragement. Before we agreed to stop getting together, she became a great, confident, skilled lover. I thoroughly enjoyed our lovemaking times together, especially toward the end.

She expressed her gratitude to me in many ways. She had expensive, custom-made jewelry delivered to me, very discreetly. She included me in her husband's hush-hush real estate deals that brought me more security and wealth than I had ever known before.

I have felt guilty sometimes since then, once in a while when I see her name in print, that she never knew how I actually got involved with her. One of my women friends had once been Joe's lover, and through her, he asked me to help him with Helena and arranged my first meeting with her. Joe knew all along what was going on—from the first time I met Helena and the first time I slid off those obscenely expensive silk panties, to the last time I kissed her gorgeous peaches-and-cream inner thighs.

Joe anonymously deposited many dollars and francs in my foreign bank accounts during the three years I was "cheating" with Helena and teaching her how to become a better lover. Lots of times he would be waiting for my call after I finished so he could rush over from one of his offices to their posh apartment and enjoy the fruits of my labors while she was still aroused and ready for him.

After all was said and done, Joe was deliriously happy with the results until Helena eventually took him to the cleaners, financially and otherwise. In their rather ugly divorce, she left him for the man she really loved, her German baron.

Thankfully, Joe never blamed me. He had the money and power to squash me like a bug, but he didn't. He blamed the baron, who has since met with several unfortunate, totally unpublicized "accidents." Better the baron than me. And, believe me, I would not mention this story, even with many of the details changed, if Joe had not passed away several years ago.

Like I said before, he could have ruined me if he'd wanted to do so—financially and physically. Instead, he was a valued friend and confidant to the end, especially when I repeated the process another time with the even younger wife who eventually inherited most of his fortune.

(5) In your opinion, what is the secret to being a seasoned, sensual senior, and what is one story you would like to tell that would help people understand how special sex can be to people over 60?

The secret to staying sexy is being healthy and active, and always learning. I do all kinds of stretching exercises every day, and I do them in the nude for added personal enjoyment, often during my private time while lying in the sun.

I know this makes it sound as if I'm the secret central character in Carly Simon's "You're So Vain," but I have mirrors on all four walls of my exercise room and indoor pool.

I jog or swim almost every day, in the nude whenever possible. I have a whole stretching regimen that I go through every morning, something I learned from a ballet dancer who was also a client. Mainly I stay in shape dancing. I love to dance, not just because I can hold a woman close—which is enough of a reward in itself, but because I like to be alive and vibrant, which dancing does to me.

I read voraciously every day. My library is filled with books that I have actually read, unlike the spacious libraries filled with unread first edition, leather-bound books in the homes of many of my wealthy friends. I subscribe to local, national and international newspapers. I've grown to absolutely love the Internet, as well, for it places the world at my fingertips.

And, yes, I read anything that will teach me to be a better lover. That doesn't mean pornography. To me, pornography is boorish and totally unrealistic. It's always about the same thing, and most of it is very degrading to women. *De trop!*

I always hated it when I was with a woman who had seen pornography and expected me to act like the coarse, underpaid, no-talent actors. Even worse is when a woman tried to make the same forced movements and noxious sounds as the coarse, underpaid, no-talent actresses.

Sex is supposed to be beautiful and uplifting. It's about romance. It's about time together and tenderness. It's about flowers and soft kisses and gentle phrases. It's about feeling two lives connect deeply. It's been that way most of my life. It is that way with my wonderful companion now. She is my most prized trophy, and I am hers.

Good sex is simply an outgrowth of everything else. It's not about monstrous size, spurting semen and artificial noises. It's not about demeaning another person, either. It's learning how to satisfy each other.

And sex at 74 continues to be a great adventure for me. I am looking forward to being married to enjoy the adventure more than ever. As with the finest wines or the best golf courses, you know nothing is ever completely perfect, though the quest for perfection and enjoyment is powerful. No matter how good it feels or how spent and satisfied you are when you are finished making love, you always feel you may be able to do it better the next time. And every time is the beginning of the next time.

Uncle Rafael said it best: "Sex, like life, is very, very good. And even when it's bad, it's good." Okay, he said it in French, and I doubt he came up with that saying, since I've heard it in many languages since then, but he was the first person I ever heard say those words. And he was right.

Even if sex is not always earth-shattering, it is always wonderful because it involves closeness and caring. I'm glad I've got to give and receive a lot of pleasure in my life, and I'm even more satisfied that I am getting a chance to do it right with the woman who will soon be my wife.

I guess it seems ironic hearing this from a man who was once a gigolo, and I certainly don't suggest than anyone else follow my example for my life—especially in today's age of diseases that kill. In fact—and I know people won't believe me after reading this story—I have become a very vocal advocate of marriage and fidelity. In today's day and age, it's the only way to guarantee a long, happy life. I didn't understand that when I was young, nor did I choose to explore the idea. Nor, during those earliest years, did I have much of a choice. I do now, though.

Yet if anything I've learned back then can help teach men to be better, more romantic lovers, and if women can enjoy the fruits of a loving husband's newfound skills, maybe my life has counted for something.

AL & ARLETTA (BOTH 74)
THE SECOND TIME AROUND

"There's a Big Band song that talks about love being lovelier the second time around. In our case, it is definitely true. I still feel like Cinderella. Al has been the best Prince Charming in the world. And I have the glass slippers to prove it!"

—ARLETTA

(1) What is your age, background and general health?

ARLETTA

Al and I are both 74. He has spent most of his life in construction, and he runs a good-sized building company in a large city in the Southwest. We've been married 10 years.

As for our background, the only way I know to explain our situation is to just jump right into it. Al and I were high school sweethearts. Actually, we were junior high sweethearts, too. I knew he was the one for me the night of our eighth-grade graduation. I think he knew it, too, and I can still remember how he walked up in a nice gray suit, starched white shirt with a red tie and matching red *boutonnière* on his suit lapel. We had been friends for several months since he moved into the area and rode on the same school bus, but that night, my heart went patter-pat, and I just thought he was the nicest looking guy in the whole school.

He surprised me by giving me a small wrapped package. In it was a silver locket with the inscription, "Special Friends." I was shocked. I had no gift to give him. Not many of our eighth grade class exchanged graduation gifts. That was more of a high school thing. But I thought it was just the nicest thing anyone could do.

Well, we didn't see much of each other that summer. I went to band camp, church camp, and to Galveston for a big family reunion. He wrote a couple of letters, and I sent him a couple of "Having a Great Time...Wish You Were Here"-type postcards. But that was about it.

We got to be better friends when our freshman year started. He was always involved in sports—football, basketball, baseball—and when he wasn't at practice or playing games, he was helping out with his Dad's construction business. We would see each other in the hallways at school, and had a few classes together, and we often ate lunch together, but that was about it. It wasn't as if either of us wanted to get too serious.

When he got a car, though, he actually started calling and asking to take me to the movies on Saturday nights or to church on Sunday mornings. Eventually, my Papa relented and after going with me to church a number of times, Al and I got to go on a real date in his shiny Chevrolet convertible. It wasn't brand new, but he sure treated it like it was pure gold. And I must admit, he always treated me that way, too.

He asked me to "go steady" the beginning of our senior year, and we actually talked about getting married someday—someday ˋway out there after each of us went to college for awhile. I planned to go to a small Christian college, and he was going to the University of Texas on a football scholarship. We pledged to save ourselves for each other.

Then we broke up as a result of a stupid teenage misunderstanding. Not long before we were both planning to leave for our respective colleges, my best girlfriend Ruthie told me that Al had been seen driving around with a girl with a bad reputation.

Then—as I discovered 30 years later— Ruthie told Al that she hated to see him being made such a fool and "confided" how I was secretly in love with someone who went to the college I was going to attend.

Al was broken hearted at the news. I was broken hearted with what I had heard about his driving around with another girl. We suddenly stopped talking to each other. I would even hang up every time he called our house. It got to the point that he came around several times with that "hang-dawg" look, as Mama described it, and I would refuse to come downstairs to talk with him.

In a last ditch attempt to clear things up before we both left for college, Al gave my girlfriend a letter in which he told what he had heard about me, and vowed that he loved me dearly, no matter what, and that he wanted us to meet and talk things through. He even gave the place and time for us to get-together.

Ruthie, to make a long story very short, never gave me the letter. Instead, she continued to fan the flames burning the bridge between Al and me.

I'm sure you know where this story is going. My best friend consoled Al through his loss, and eventually stopped communicating with me. Eventually, she followed Al to Austin. On Saturday afternoons she wore burnt orange and cheered him on to football glory. Not long after they both graduated, Al and Ruthie got married there on the campus.

Mama sent me a copy of the newspaper story about their wedding. I tore it up and threw it away.

Sadly, I hadn't seen any of it coming, especially my girlfriend's betrayal, but after high school graduation I decided to make the best of it. I left for college and spent the next four years as a full-time student.

The next 30 years went by in a blur. I married a ministerial student named John, we had four children and held pastorates in five different West Texas churches. Then my husband was tragically killed in an airplane crash not long after our silver wedding anniversary celebration.

A year after my husband's death, my children talked me into going to my high school's thirtieth anniversary. After some arm-twisting, I did go. Al surprised me by showing up, too, then asking me to dance with him—"One time for old time's sake." Red-faced and angry, I turned to walk away from him, but he quickly said, "You believed a lie about me back then. Won't you at least listen to the truth now?"

I had no idea what he was talking about.

"A lie?" I asked.

He nodded, then led me to a table for two. For the next half-hour, it was if no one else was around us. Ruthie, his wife and once my best friend, had passed away a year before after a long bout with cancer. Not long before she went, she told him exactly what had happened—her lies, the torn-up letter, what she had told me about him, everything.

I was flabbergasted. I wanted to be angry at someone, but couldn't be mad at a dead person, and I no longer had a reason to be mad at Al. Maybe I was simply mad at myself for believing Ruthie rather than confronting Al directly about the gossip.

It was if a huge puzzle piece was suddenly lifted into place which answered a 30-year mystery that had changed the lives of so many people, yet the gaping cavern inside me that I kept trying to ignore only seemed more bewildering.

He asked me about my life. I shared what had happened with John and me. Even as we talked, I was increasingly aware of the sadness I was feeling that I had kept bottled up for years.

Al told me of the many times, especially during his marriage, he had felt guilty for wondering how much different it might have been.

We talked for some time. Danced together once—one time for old time's sake—as Al has originally asked. We both promised to get back together for lunch if I came back to the hometown anytime soon. Then we said our goodbyes and I left.

I guess it would have made a great ending if we would have fallen in each other's arms that night and lived happily ever after, but it didn't happen that way. For one thing, we both had our own families and lives and memories with our spouses that each of us felt loyal to.

I told him how wonderful it was that we had been able to clear the air, so to speak, but when I told him "Goodbye," I knew I was closing the door on a lifetime of what-could-have-beens, and I vowed to myself to never look back.

Unfortunately, my heart didn't go along with the plan in my head. It was perhaps a week later that I collapsed on my bed, sobbing at everything that had taken place, crying uncontrollably for some time. It was so unlike me, and that especially scared me.

I've heard it said that your first love always owns a piece of your heart. I had lived a wonderful life and had enjoyed a beautiful marriage with my husband John, but there were those secret times when I took out the "Special Friends" silver locket he had given me at our eighth grade graduation and wondered what Al was doing. There were even times that I prayed for him, Ruthie, and their family—wherever they were and whatever they were doing.

It wasn't as it I spent 30 years dwelling on him or moping around because of what took place. I loved my husband, children and grandchildren, and I couldn't imagine life going any other direction. But, still, there was always that secret soft spot for him, I suppose.

AL

I can't say I was quite as forgiving. For 30 years I had kept a jagged chunk of hate bottled up inside me toward Arletta for what I thought she had done to me.

Sure, I had got on with my life, made the best of the situation, had a very rewarding college football career, eventually married Ruthie, and we had four great children and a growing number of grandchildren. Still, I could never understand why every attempt to explain what had happened between Arletta and me had been totally ignored by her after being so much in love. It was a festering wound inside my heart. I wanted to let go of it, but I was never quite able to do so. I heard about her and her husband from time to time, but despised the ground she walked on for ditching me for some preacher-boy.

When Ruthie—quite literally on her death-bed—finally did tell me everything that had really happened when we were back in high school, I had no realistic way to deal with it except to suck it up and be a man. Certainly I couldn't take it out on my dying wife. She felt overwhelmed with grief at what she had done and was trying to clear up what she had done. How could I not forgive her, especially at that moment?

My life with her had not always been per-fect, as no marriage is, but we had built a good life together, and I always prided myself on being a stand-up guy with my obligations. All along, back when we had only been mar-ried a few years and I knew I could never feel for Ruthie like I had once loved Arletta, I still believed that I owed it to Ruthie and our kids to stay married and keep up all the appearances. Maybe it seems like something from a lost generation, but "love, honor and cherish" was supposed to mean something, even if I didn't always feel like being married anymore. That was the honor system I lived by.

After Ruthie passed away, I was numb for several months. I guess it all came to a head one night. There were no kids or grandkids around that evening. I was all alone. I became a living, breathing Merle Haggard song.

I never drank much my entire life except for a few partying years while I was in college. But that evening I felt 10 ways of sorry for myself, so I went to a nearby liquor store, bought a bottle of Jack Daniels Black, drove out to Ruthie's gravesite and got roaring drunk listening to an oldies country music station. All the drinkin' and hurtin' songs made me feel even worse, which is exactly what I wanted. I felt dead inside and anything, even hurt, was preferable to feeling nothing at all.

I don't remember much of anything else until I came to, realizing I had crawled on my hands and knees to her grave and was pounding on the sod, screaming into the vast darkness all the things I wish I could have told my late wife when she was alive, especially about how she had lied to both me and Arletta, changing all of our lives forever.

Sure, it was crazy. Yeah, I was totally out of my head with grief. But in a strange way, it allowed me to get some things released from a heart that had become hard as quartz.

I don't remember much else. I passed out while lying on Ruthie's grave. I woke up with the whiskey bottle smashed against the gravestone and my knuckles bloody, I suppose from bashing them into the ground and possibly the headstone, as well. The country music was still blasting from my pick-up, and it was that song, "One Day at a Time."

Even then, hung over and my hands throbbing, I thought the song playing at that exact moment was no small coincidence. The sunrise shone all around me. Something was different. It was as if I had faced down all the shadowy demons in my heart and would live to see another day.

I walked over to my pickup, and a quick glance in the rearview mirror of my pickup brought me down to earth. For someone who was basking in the sunshine of a new day, I looked like death warmed over.

Looking back, I'm really glad no one saw me there at the gravesite that night, screaming and cursing at a dead person's grave. And I hope no one drove past that morning before

I woke up. No one ever mentioned anything to me if they did. Or if they did, maybe they just thought I was overcome with grief. In a real way, I was. I was grieving the loss of two women in my life, and there didn't seem to be anything I could do about anything.

I downloaded that song that had been playing when I gained consciousness, and I started playing "One Day at a Time" often in my pickup or at the house whenever I felt depressed or filled with self-pity, which hap- pened pretty regularly. The song was kinda like a prayer. In fact I read a book later about the Nashville writer, Marijohn Wilkin, and the story behind the song.

It was a prayer for her after her life had blown to bits and she tried to kill herself. But on an Easter morning back in the Sixties, she realized that she had lived to face another day, and sat down at a piano to tell God what she was feeling. Later her buddy Kris Kristofferson helped add a verse, but the core of the song was what actually happened to her.

Even before I knew all that about the song, her words spoke directly to my soul— about taking responsibility for me and all the choices I had made in life, as well as being grateful for the good things I did have. And it seemed hopeful, sort of like Crystal Gayle's

"Ready for the Times to Get Better," another old country tune that I played over and over. I needed a boatload of hope during those days as I tried to sort things out, and those two songs became very important to regaining my life.

I can honestly say, though I wouldn't recommend the grave scene to anyone else, that from that moment, I started to heal inside. It a weird way, what I did worked for me. And the whole process proved to be a hell of a lot cheaper than a room full of psychologists it would have taken to break through the stonewall fortress I had built up inside me!

But that's not all of the story. Ironically, that same morning after I woke up at Ruthie's grave and heard "One Day at a Time" playing on the radio, I headed back to my house to get cleaned up and to get ready to go to one of my job sites. As I got out of the shower, I flipped on the television in my bedroom, and the tragic news of a small aircraft crashing not far from my home place was hitting the local news. There had been no survivors. The plane had been heading from a small nearby airport to West Texas. I don't know why, but even at that moment I had this eerie feeling in my heart that the crash was significant in some way. I had a lot of friends and business associates who flew small planes, and I wondered if it could be any of them. I listened and watched a bit more as I got dressed, but I didn't hear any more details.

Later that day, when the authorities released the name of the deceased, a chill ran down my back. The name, especially since he was called "Reverend," was the same as Arletta's husband John. He was a beloved pastor out in West Texas, so the news flashed around the state.

Even though I didn't know him personally, I felt like someone had punched me in the gut. In a strange way, it was as if I had lost a close friend or family member, though those feelings made no sense at all.

I wished I could do something, but had no idea what to do. I didn't feel right contacting Arletta, since she still believed all the things Ruthie had told her. I thought about sending flowers to the funeral home, or maybe even flying out to West Texas to go to the funeral, but that seemed ill-advised with what had happened so long ago. I certainly didn't want to cause any problems during a time of grief that I had gone through myself, so in the end, I did nothing.

I do remember offering up a few prayers for Arletta and her family. And I remember praying specifically that someday I would have the opportunity to make things right, though that seemed about as likely as me flying to the moon without a rocket.

In the months before our thirtieth class reunion, I wondered about even going. As our senior class president, even after three decades, I was expected to make an appearance and say a few things. I doubted that Arletta would be there, especially with the death of her husband so recently, but I actually planned what I might say to her in case she did come to the reunion. No matter what else happened, I simply kept hoping against hope that I could at least clear the air between us, all the time knowing full well that `way too much water had gone under the bridge for us to ever be friends again.

Unfortunately, when I finally saw her that night at the dance, the sight of her literally took my breath away. My knees almost buckled, it was that emotional. I'm good at running a bluff, both in cards and in life, so no one would have noticed what I was feeling at that moment. But I knew.

Suddenly, when the big moment happened, I simply couldn't remember a word of the well-planned speech I'd prepared in my mind. I felt like a drowning man sucking water with no hope and no rope. Finally I spoke totally out of desperation.

I'm so glad she finally agreed to sit with me for a moment. I felt as if I would burst if she didn't know the truth—despite what might happen.

After she left that night, I knew I had failed. I had gotten one chance to make things right, and I had obviously blown it. I went out to Ruthie's grave again that night, but I didn't drink anything. Or say anything. Or feel much of anything. I didn't even walk over to the gravesite, but just sat in the pickup in the silence, looking up at the stars, surrounded by the night sounds. I sat there for a long, long time.

Finally, resigned to the future, whatever it was, I started up my pickup, turned up "One Day at a Time," and drove home to begin my life all over. Without Ruthie. Without Arletta. Without any hope of clearing the air with Arletta.

As usual, I knew I had to man up and get on with my life. My kids and grandkids certainly didn't need to see me moping around, especially after the sadness of losing their Mom and Grandma Ruthie. And my construction business clients and workers were all depending on me to keep everything going.

Imagine my surprise when Arletta wrote me a few days later, thanking me for taking the time to talk with her and asking my forgiveness for believing Ruthie's lies.

She wanted *me* to forgive *her*! I couldn't believe my eyes. I was the one who needed forgiveness, not her.

That began a hopeful season of writing heartfelt letters and occasional phone calls. I was hesitant to say what I was really feeling, fearful that she would suddenly stop writing or phoning.

I was willing to do anything, even keeping everything rather distant, just to have some kind of contact with her. I hated the thought of the door closing out another failed chapter of our lives.

Eventually, hope began to grow. It became more obvious that a warm friendship was forming. Frankly, that's about all I was ready for at that point. Probably her, too. In my case, not only was the construction business in our area in the throes of a major down-turn, running parallel with a tough time for the oil business, but I just wasn't emotion-ally prepared to start anything new with any-one, in terms of a relationship. I was still pretty much a basket case after my marriage to Ruthie, her death, and the way it had all ended with her, but I was thankfully learn-ing to take life one day at a time, just like the song said.

Thankfully, in the end, I didn't have to start anything new. In many ways, Arletta and I had resumed something that had been pure and wonderful and warm more than three decades before it was broken. Though it had been ripped apart by gossip and lies, the solid pieces were still there in our hearts.

To put all those smashed fragments together quickly, rather than drawing this out for you and boring you to tears, let me just say that it took a year after we met at that class reunion to actually start spending any time together. It took some doing to make sure both her family and my family would accept what seemed to be happening.

Two years to the day from the night of the class reunion, my sweetheart Arletta and I stood at the front of a beautiful church in our hometown, the same place we used to attend together on Sundays as teenagers, and vowed to love, honor and cherish from that day forward. I could barely say the words for the lump in my throat, and when we kissed after being pronounced man and wife, I finally let go and cried big ole tears of heartache and loss mingled with the most wonderful joy and unbelievable gratefulness.

Arletta was crying, too. Our families and friends were weeping. Here we were on the happiest day either of us had experienced for some time, and we were bawling like babies. I don't think there were many dry eyes in the place.

Even the preacher joined in and had to pull out his handkerchief to wipe away the tears.

I wish I had words to describe how good it has been since then. All I know is that I feel like God gave us a second chance at love, and I want to make the most of this gift He's given us for as long as possible.

(2) Is sex still a part of your life, and, if so, how has it (and you) changed over the years?

AL

It is. Sex has always been important to me. There were some times of petting when we were teenagers, but Arletta and I never went all the way. After all that happened, the break-up and all, I'm glad we didn't. At the time, though, it was almost more than I could handle to be with her, dream about her, think about her, lust after her, and yet knew that neither of us really wanted to go much farther.

After Arletta left for college and I headed for Austin, I got a little crazy for awhile. I dated Ruthie some, since she was at UT, too, but I went pretty wild. I didn't plan to.

In fact, I didn't even drink when I first headed to college. But one night, not long after practice started, a bunch of my team-mates headed out to get some beer and pizza, and they asked me to go along. I went, hungry for some food and wanting to hang out with my new teammates, but not wanting to get in trouble with the coaches for being out past our curfew.

At the pizza café not far from the campus, everything was getting a little rowdy and everyone was having a good time. Then one of the upperclassmen, a 275-pound offensive lineman, saw that I wasn't guzzling beer like the rest of them. He picked up a full pitcher, walked over where I was sitting, poured me a mug full, and motioned for me to chug it down. I shook my head, not wanting to make a scene.

"I don't want to mess up my training," I said hesitantly. "I...I don't really drink beer."

I'll never forget the line he thundered: "Drink it or you'll wear it!"

It was as if the entire place was suddenly bathed in silence. I could actually hear a clock ticking somewhere on a wall. I knew he'd do what he said, and I would end up going back into the jock's dorm reeking of beer. Back in those days, especially if you were a freshman, you could get kicked off the team and knocked out of a scholarship.

So I made a choice that affected me for a long time. I caved. Drank the beer. Drank another when he repeated his threat. And another. By the time we all staggered back to the dorm together, I was just another one of the boys. It was pretty much that way for the next two years. If the team headed to the famous Chicken Ranch and invited me, I went along. If they headed down to Mexico for a spring break, I went along and tried to drink the place dry along with the rest of 'em. It's a pure wonder how I kept from catching some dreaded disease or becoming a total alcoholic. It's not as if I didn't give it the old college try.

About the time I entered my junior year, I decided I needed to get my act together. Football had pretty much been my life, but I already knew that I might be a good college player, but I was a step too slow and 40 pounds too small to have a chance in the NFL.

I actually selected a real major instead of "undecided," and I got serious about something other than partying and goofing around in my spare time. It's about that time that I decided that since it would never work out with Arletta, my first love, that I'd start looking elsewhere besides one night stands. Ruthie was always there, and we started gravitating toward each other more and more.

Right after both of us graduated, we had a nice wedding at chapel near the campus. Her parents and mine both owed big construction businesses and were good friends, so it all seemed to fit together.

Ruthie and I had been sexually active, on and off, during our college years. During our honeymoon, the sex mainly meant no fears of getting pregnant anymore. Good thing. She conceived within hours of us saying "I do."

I got busy helping my dad in his construction business. Our family started growing. We joined the family's church, the right civic clubs, and the proper organizations. Ruthie and I were both elected to this office or that leadership position. Our kids' activities made life more and more of a blur. Before long, we were locked into a lifestyle that really didn't allow me much time to confront the feelings that something was wrong. Desperately wrong.

Sex was okay, but it was replaced with some kind of unemotional imitation. I take the blame for it. I just never felt very close to Ruthie. I don't think she ever cheated on me, and I never cheated on her. Still, it just never was more than a mechanical sex act. We tried. We went to marriage counseling. We got the funky sex toy catalogs and tried to spice things up. We went on vacations without the kids as we got older, hoping to discover whatever-it-was that was missing from our relationship.

Nothing.

I guess the saddest thing I ever remember hearing, right before she died, was Ruthie saying, "Al, I've known all along—deep down—that you never really loved me as much as I loved you. I just thought I could love enough for the both of us."

The worse thing is that I knew she had hit the nail on the head. I wanted it to not be true. I had tried to prove my love for Ruthie all our life together. But it was true what she said. And I felt like the most horrible excuse for a man I could be at that moment. I had lived a lie, and Ruthie had known it all along.

She died two days later. At that moment I held her hand, feeling as if the world we had created was crumbling apart and there wasn't a damn thing I could do about it.

(3) If you are currently involved in an intimate relationship, how long has it lasted? What has made it last? What have been the best (or worse) parts of the relationship?

ARLETTA

Hearing Al say that about himself and Arletta brings such tears to my eyes. There were so many times I felt the same way—that I was living a lie. I sometimes searched for some sort of signal in my husband's eyes, wondering if he could sense what I felt, deep inside. He either never saw it, or else he was simply too wonderful of a man to confront me with it.

Our sex life was always good. He was a perfect gentleman, never pushed me to do anything I didn't want to do and encouraged me in every way. In fact, I was often the pursuer. As I got more confident, I discovered more and more what I especially liked him to do, and I liked to find ways to make it better for him. It was good.

Our schedules were always so busy, especially as the children got older and went to scouts, little league, youth groups, vacation Bible schools and sports. Still, we always tried to be a couple, first and foremost. I'm not sure we always succeeded, but it wasn't for a lack of love.

When he died in the plane crash, I honestly felt as if my life was gone, too. I never imagined for a moment that I would ever be with anyone else. And being with Al was probably the farthest thing from my mind.

I guess that's why our life now—Al and me—is such a pleasant surprise. Of course we've both had to sort things out, especially our feelings for our spouses and what we increasingly felt for each other. Still, even that first night at the class reunion, there was something very warm and familiar about being with Al again.

By the time Al and we were married, so many of my sexual feelings had returned. I'm embarrassed to say it, even though I trust you to change enough details that none of my friends or family will recognize me through this interview, but I was almost insatiable on my honeymoon with Al. It was as if I couldn't get enough of him. Maybe I was subconsciously thinking that I would lose him again. Maybe I was making up for lost time with him. Whatever the cause was, I was almost beside myself in bed with him. It scared me because I had never quite felt this way.

I got a bit sidetracked, but I wanted to let you know that we haven't sat around brooding our lives away with "what-might-have-beens" since we've been back together. We've been married nearly 10 years now. I can honestly say that it has been very good, sexually and all the other ways. I feel very blessed.

(4) What details about you, your partner and your sexual relationship would surprise people if they knew?

ARLETTA

I think if people knew how much both of us enjoy each other sexually, even after 10 years of being together, it would definitely be a surprise. I think the good appetite for lovemaking is certainly tied to living a healthy and fit lifestyle. And I'm sure it has something to do with being back together after three decades of being apart.

AL

A long time ago I heard an old West Texas rancher say, "If I knew I was a-gonna live this long, I'd a taken better care of myself." I've sometimes felt that way, even though I've always been active. And it definitely relates to sex and romance.

Neither of us was ever horribly out of shape, but both Arletta and I had started letting ourselves go some and not taking as good care of ourselves during the times of grieving and loss. Even before we got married, we started challenging each other to eat better and exercise more, not out of meddling, but both of us acutely aware that we wanted to cherish the coming years together.

One of the good things about our bodies is that it is never too late to take better care of yourself and live healthy, not as long as you're still breathing. I'm living proof of that.

As Arletta said, even before we got married, we made up our minds to enjoy our time together to the fullest and to be as healthy as possible for each other.

It wasn't easy, getting in better shape. It still isn't. But the rewards so far outweigh the other alternatives in so many ways.

I really like being slimmer, more fit. I like how feeling younger translates to being better in bed. I'm almost embarrassed to say it this way, but you even look bigger sexually when you become more fit. I doubt there's a man in the world that doesn't like that, regardless of age, I can guarantee you!

Sex has been great with us. Sure, it took a little bit of adjustment at first. It was awkward, having spent our adult lives with others. Neither knew what the other liked or expected. Frankly, on our honeymoon night, I felt like a nervous teenager, kinda like doing it for the first time. I wanted it to be so good for both of us.

I can say this now, though I have never even told Arletta what I'm about to say. I almost wept the moment I went inside her for the first time. It was as if I had waited my whole life to feel what I was feeling with her. The most uncontrollable emotions were racing through me. And I'm not exactly known for being the emotional type. In fact, I always considered myself pretty damn tough. One time in college I played most of the final game of the season on a broken ankle, and no one knew about it until after the game was over. Unfortunately we lost the game and the season was over, but nothing or nobody was going to get to me when I decided to tough things out.

As I've said before, I can run a bluff with the best of `em, but that macho stuff went out the window on both our wedding day and especially on our first honeymoon night when I began thinking about how much of a miracle it was for us to be where we were at that exact moment.

Now, I've always believed that a gentleman doesn't kiss and tell, so this is a little hard for me now. I'm only doing this because I know you will clean it up and make it so people can't recognize us.

When we made love for the first time, I can remember how it felt with each stroke. I felt it all through my body. It was simply the greatest sensation. It looked like Arletta was enjoying it, too. I loved the sounds she made. Then as I stroked harder, she began arching her back and pushing against me more and more, her breaths getting deeper and deeper.

We climaxed together that very first time, just like in some kind of erotic storybook. It was almost more than I could take. It was that good. They say waiting always makes sex special. In some ways I had waited 30-some years to be this close to Arletta. Every place that our skin touched, it felt like the most wonderful, sensual sensation.

It was as if all the emotions of a lifetime were pent up inside and exploding at the same time we were climaxing together. I don't know if that makes sense to you or not, but it's as real to me as if it happened yesterday. I can't even begin to describe how wonderful it was for me. We have never talked so openly about that first time before, so I can only hope it was as good for her as it was for me. It's almost like I never wanted to talk about it before, as if it would detract from how really good it was.

Not many people get to experience great sex at 64 for the first time with a woman they have known and loved deeply since junior high. I felt blessed that first honeymoon night as we fell asleep in each other's arms. It felt so right, so natural. Ten years later, I still feel that way with her.

(5) In your opinion, what is the secret to being a seasoned, sensual senior and what is one story you would like to tell

that would help people understand how special sex can be to people over 60?

ARLETTA

Whew! I don't know what the secret is. We've mentioned being in good shape. That's part of it. Having a good attitude about life helps. So is making the decision to enjoy our moments together, knowing how fleeting life can be.

As for a particularly special time to show how good sex can be for people our age—there is one that especially stands out because it was just so amazing.

I'm pretty good at remembering details, but I'm sure this will go on and on since it is such a wonderful memory. You can cut out anything that makes it too long or boring to other people.

A couple of years ago Al called me and asked if I would ride over to a construction site one evening. It was a large building in the downtown area of the city where we live, and nearly completed, except for the top couple of stories. When we got there, everyone had already left the site except for the security man. Al grabbed a couple of briefcases from his pickup, came around and opened my door, then asked me to follow him. I heard him tell the security man that we were going inside for awhile to check out progress on the project. I could have sworn that the security guy grinned, but it was probably just my imagination. We walked inside the lobby, and Al punched the number for the top floor.

When we walked out of the elevator, almost all of the lights were off, but I could see well enough to follow him as he made his way to a closed door, which led to a flight of steps, which led to the roof of the building.

I'm not really afraid of heights, but I'm not crazy about them, either. When we walked out onto the roof, I was overtaken with the beauty. The panorama all around us was breathtaking. What a gorgeous sunset!

Stories below, the vehicles were moving and people walking. No one could see us, but it seemed we were watching over the entire city from where we stood, except for an area that had a red-velvet looking curtain around it.

Al closed the door behind us and pad-locked it. When I asked him why, he just put a finger to his lips and motioned for me to walk with him toward the curtained area.

Inside, totally hidden to me before, was a beautiful, polished dining table and chairs, covered with the most gorgeous lace table-cloth and silverware I had ever seen. It had a candelabra with a dozen long, narrow tapers.

Surprisingly for our part of Texas, there was very little breeze that night, and the candles were flickering gently. Al took off his hard-hat, bowed gracefully, and held a chair for me to be seated.

He went inside the curtained area. Momentarily, he wheeled out a table with a nice CD stereo player on it. He touched a couple of buttons, and Glenn Miller's "String of Pearls" began. That song always starts with a big blast of brass horns, and it startled me until I realized what it was. I couldn't remember telling him—though I must have—but that song had always been one of my favorite songs since I was a little girl.

And he was just beginning. He quickly tugged at his work shirt, pulling if off to reveal a tuxedo shirt and tie underneath. Then he pulled off his boots, then his pants, only to show me that had a cummerbund and black tuxedo pants underneath. He went behind the curtains and returned quickly with a white jacket and shiny black shoes on.

I started to joke that I was obviously under-dressed for the occasion, but he put a finger to my mouth and walked to the curtained area again. He emerged carrying a large box and helped me open it. It was the most gorgeous red satin gown!

He stood me up, draped the gown over my chair, and proceeded to undress me, right down to my panties and brassiere. I worried at first that someone might see me, but looked around in every direction and assured myself that no one could see us up so high. He helped me into my gown. It fit perfectly, and I felt like Cinderella on my throne as I sat down again. That had always been my favorite childhood story, but I doubted he would remember that.

Wouldn't you know it? No sooner had I thought of the name Cinderella, than he went into the curtained area and came back with another box. He knelt before me to pull out a pair of glass slippers. I swear! They weren't really glass, but they were shiny, transparent and very expensive-looking.

At that moment, I was Cinderella!

Then, my own Prince Charming got another smaller box and brought it to me. I took the bow off and opened it. It was the most beautiful pearl necklace I swear I had ever seen!

I noticed that Al had the stereo set on "repeat" so the CD kept playing "String of Pearls" over and over. He helped me clasp the necklace around my neck, then took my hands and began dancing slowly.

I hope it didn't show on my face, but I was in such shock at the surroundings and all he was doing that I couldn't bring myself to say anything. I just kept looking at him, then leaning my head against him and dancing, then looking back at him. I wondered what else he had prepared.

Actually, he had a whole lot prepared. After dancing awhile, he sat me down and left for a moment, went behind the curtain, and promptly wheeled out a serving cart. All my favorite foods had been prepared by God-only-knows-who, right down to the endive salad and Beef Wellington! I could not believe what was happening. I just hoped that no midnight chimes would sound and make it all disappear.

We danced more that night. I kept feeling and looking at my necklace and gown, still unable to fathom how wonderful my life had become with this man in so many unexpected ways.

I reached a point where I was almost beside myself with passion for him. Maybe it is unbecoming for someone my age to talk about things like this, but it was as if I had a roaring fire inside. I couldn't wait for him to make love to me.

He reached over and opened the curtained area beside us for me to see inside. It was decorated like a romantic *boudoir* from some romance novel set in the nineteenth century.

I needed him desperately and grappled frantically with his zipper. We made love fully clothed.

Thankfully, "String of Pearls" kept playing over and over, otherwise the entire downtown area would have heard one very excited lady moaning rather loudly!

At some point, he got up and switched the music to the same Glenn Miller CD playing "Stairway to the Stars." Like "Sting of Pearls," it was another perfect song for the most memorable of moments. The whole city was bathed with stars. We listened to the song several times, then he finally turned it off and we fell asleep, still fully clothed, lying in each other's arms.

Thankfully, Al had told his crew not to report for work until 10 the next morning. By that time we had watched the sunrise together as we held each other tightly, drank freshly brewed coffee and warm croissants that mysteriously appeared from behind the padlocked door. Then we headed home in his pickup. By 10 o'clock, as his crew started arriving at the construction site, Al and I were already home, taking a dip in the pool, toweling each other off and holding each other close.

I hope he keeps surprising me and making love to me for years to come. We both understand that we don't have a guaranteed tomorrow, so we are passionate about enjoying every moment, one day at a time.

It's like the old Frank Sinatra song that sometimes seems as if it were written for Al and me:

> Love is lovelier, the second time around
> Just as wonderful, with both feet on the ground
> It's that second time you hear your love song sung
> Makes you think perhaps that love, like youth,
> > is wasted on the young
>
> Love's more comfortable the second time you fall
> Like a friendly home the second time you call
> Who can say, what brought us to this miracle we've found?
>
> There are those who'd bet
> Love comes but once, and yet
> I'm oh so glad we met
> The second time around[5*]

---

5   * Sammy Cahn and Jimmy Van Heusen, Warner/Chappell Music Publishing, Used by permission.

I still feel like Cinderella who got a second time around with my first love. I thought my life was over nearly 12 years ago. Al entered my life again as Prince Charming and has made everything into a wonderful fairy tale. And I still have my glass slippers—I've kept them in a special showcase in our bedroom to remember that night on top of the world!

Who could have ever guessed it would turn out this way after 30 years apart for a couple of high school sweethearts?

A FINAL NOTE

Your Own Seasoned Romance™ Questionnaire

Now that you have completed the book, we encourage you to let us know what you think about the interviews and ideas you have read. Also, if you would like to receive information concerning future books in this series, please check DeLeeuw Research Group at DeLeeuwResearch.com or FirePointe.com.

You can also purchase both soft-cover and digital copies of all the Seasoned Romance™ series books at such online retailers as Amazon.com, as well as your local bookstores.

Better yet, perhaps you would like to participate in the ongoing study which focuses on what we can learn from an even wider range of Seniors. As we go to print with the first Seasoned Romance Book One, we are already making plans to develop future projects.

If you would like to participate in the continuing study (you and/or your partner should be 60 years old or older to be able to participate), please go to our website to complete the following five questions (or you can send your answers typed, handwritten, or on an audio cassette/CD to the address at the end of this section):

SEASONED ROMANCE™ QUESTIONNAIRE®

(1) What is your age, background and general health?

(2) Is sex still a part of your life, and, if so, how has it (and you) changed over the years?

(3) If you are currently involved in an intimate relationship, how long has it lasted? What has made it last? What have been the best (or worse) parts of the relationship?

(4) What details about you, your partner and your relationship would surprise people if they knew?

(5) In your opinion, what is the secret to being a seasoned, sensual senior, and what is one story you would like to tell that would help people understand how special sex can be to people over 60?

Seasoned Romance™ Questionnaire®
Copyright ©1972–2011
by DeLeeuw Research Group.
All Rights Reserved. International Copyright Secured.
No portion of this Questionnaire may be reproduced in any form
without prior written permission from DeLeeuw Research Group.

Please send your completed questionnaire or comments via email to questionnaire@ FirePointe.com, or send mail to:

DeLeeuw Research Group
PO Box 610231
Dallas, TX 75261-0231

If you are chosen for inclusion in future books of the Seasoned Romance™ series, a schedule for additional interviews and remuneration will be discussed fully, with written agreement, prior to participation and/or books going to print.

Both now and during coming days, we wish you love, laughter, purpose, God's favor, and a lifetime filled with Seasoned Romance™!

WATCH FOR MORE GREAT BOOKS
AS THE SEASONED ROMANCE™ SERIES CONTINUES

Order paperback or Kindle® digital
copies from **Amazon.com.**

Paperback copies are also available
through top bookseller Websites,
fine bookstores in your area,
FirePointe.com and
DeLeeuwResearch.com.

Watch for more books coming soon in the Seasoned Romance series!